THE WILL OF THE PEOPLE

MARTIN GILBERT

THE WILL

OF THE

PEOPLE

*Winston Churchill
    and Parliamentary Democracy*

VINTAGE CANADA

COPYRIGHT © 2006 MARTIN GILBERT UNLIMITED

Vintage Canada and colophon are trademarks.

www.randomhouse.ca

Library and Archives Canada Cataloguing in Publication

Gilbert, Martin, 1936–
The will of the people : Churchill and parliamentary
democracy / Martin Gilbert.

ISBN-13: 978-0-679-31469-1
ISBN-10: 0-679-31469-5

1. Churchill, Winston, 1871–1947. 2. Great Britain—Politics
and government—20th century. 3. Representative government
and representation—Great Britain—History—20th century.
4. Democracy—Great Britain—History—20th century. I. Title.

DA566.9.C5G58 2006   321.8092   C2006-901615-1

Cover and text design: CS Richardson

Printed and bound in Canada

10 9 8 7 6 5 4 3 2 1

"We accept in the fullest sense of the word the settled and persistent will of the people. All this idea of a group of supermen and super-planners . . . making the masses of the people do what they think is good for them, without any check or correction, is a violation of democracy."

—Winston S. Churchill, House of Commons,
11 November 1947

THE CHURCHILL BIOGRAPHY
Volumes by Martin Gilbert

CONTENTS

1

First Steps

Parliamentary democracy is an easy concept to grasp but a difficult one to sustain. Throughout the twentieth century, and into our present twenty-first century, the institutions and ideals of parliamentary democracy have been under continual threat. The power of totalitarian regimes to dominate their own people is—and remains—attractive to those who wish to control the life of a nation without checks and balances.

In Europe, for many decades of the twentieth century, Communism, Fascism and Nazism ruled through small elites, backed by secret police to ensure their dominance. An independent judiciary and a free press were both anathema to the rulers. In the twenty-first century, these democratic values, which are universal in their implications for the quality of life and fulfilment of each person on the planet, are still under threat in many lands.

Dictatorships of one form or another continue to control their people in many of the countries of the United Nations. The world's most populous country, China, is a closed society. Fundamentalist Islamic nations adhere to anti-democratic norms. The rule of law and the rights of the individual are upheld in only a minority of the countries on the globe. Yet these principles have their champions everywhere, even in prison camps and under house arrest.

Parliamentary democracy celebrates diversity and dissent. It seeks to exclude no one from the benefits and protections of citizenship. Today, as in every decade in the past, its basic tenets are under threat: the male and female electoral franchise, the cut and thrust of parliamentary debate, the value of peaceful public criticism and opposition, the evolution of practical and egalitarian legislation, and, above all, the belief in impartial justice and the right of every adult citizen to determine his or her own destiny. The twin pillars of parliamentary democracy are the secret ballot and open debate.

More than a hundred years ago, this same system of parliamentary democracy, facing similar threats as it does today, including the apathy of those who are its beneficiaries, was championed by Winston Churchill. He was the scion not only of an aristocratic British lineage but also, on his mother's side, of an American heritage. He was only twenty-five years old when he first entered Parliament and eighty-nine when he left it.

By far the largest part of Churchill's life—of his working days and nights—was spent in the interchange of parliamentary debate. Legislation and the governance of Britain were his constant companions, the objects of his persistent work and evolving expertise. Elections and electioneering were part of his life-blood. His fellow parliamentarians were among his closest, lifelong friends.

Throughout his long life, Churchill considered the people to be sovereign, through Parliament, in deciding the destiny of the nation. During more than fifty years of political life, he did his utmost to ensure that the efforts of Parliament were effective and that its will was not undermined or bypassed.

The defeat of the Conservative Party in the General Election of 1945, which ended his wartime premiership, in no way altered Churchill's faith in parliamentary democracy or its procedures. Reflecting on his defeat the day after the results were known, he told a small gathering of family and friends: "It is the will of the people."

Not only did Churchill serve as a parliamentarian for more than half a century but he faced the electorate and campaigned for election or re-election eighteen times. In five of those campaigns he was unsuccessful. Those five defeats—the first, in 1899, a year before he entered Parliament—did not deter him. Nor did the defeat, twice, of his party, first in 1922 (the Liberal Party, of which he was a stalwart), and then in 1945 (the Conservative Party, of which he was then leader). Indeed, each of these defeats spurred him on to make effective use of the democratic and parliamentary process, to make democracy work.

For just over five years during the Second World War, Churchill headed an all-party coalition. Within it, Conservative, Liberal and Labour politicians all had important positions in every aspect of his administration, from the War Cabinet to the running of government departments. His path to the leadership of these combined political forces—hitherto almost always beset by disagreement—had begun almost forty years earlier, in 1901, shortly after the death of Queen Victoria. That year, after six crowded years as a soldier and journalist, he entered the House of Commons. From that moment, he was first and foremost a parliamentarian: a supporter, practitioner and upholder of parliamentary democracy and the rule of law.

————

Even before he entered Parliament, Churchill knew, and had become steeped in, many aspects of the parliamentary world. When he was nine years old, Woodstock, the parliamentary constituency represented by his father, Lord Randolph Churchill, was abolished. It was one of the notorious "rotten boroughs" whose electorate was small and controlled by the local landlord: in this case, his grandfather, the seventh Duke of Marlborough. Lord Randolph had therefore to find a constituency with an independent electorate. He chose to fight a largely radical Birmingham seat and, defiantly, to raise the flag of Tory Democracy there.

The young Churchill watched this process with fascination. When his headmaster's wife visited the Midlands, Churchill wrote to his mother, "they were betting two to one that Papa would get in for Birmingham." Lord Randolph was indeed successful. The concept of Tory Democracy, whereby Conservative Party policy could encompass all classes in the nation, was one that attracted the young Churchill. It enshrined one of his basic understandings of parliamentary democracy: that no one class, no one interest—economic, social or political—no one segment of the political spectrum could use the system for its own exclusive interests.

At the centre of Churchill's lifelong involvement in, and pugnacious support for, the parliamentary system was his familiarity and fascination with it from an early age. As a schoolboy in Brighton, aged ten, Churchill reported enthusiastically to his father that he had been out riding with a man "who thinks that Gladstone is a brute" and that "the one with the curly moustache"— Lord Randolph—"ought to be Premier." After Gladstone's defeat at the election of 1884, Lord Randolph became Secretary of State for India. Two years later, the Conservatives were defeated and the Liberals returned to power. When the young Churchill's pocket money was cut, he is said to have remarked: "We're out of office— and they're economising on me." When the Conservatives returned to power in 1886, his father became Chancellor of the Exchequer. An uncle, Edward Marjoribanks, was emerging as a leading Liberal. The world of Parliament, across the political divide, was part of his upbringing.

British history, with its story of the evolution of parliamentary democracy from the Magna Carta to the 1832 Reform Bill, was the subject at which Churchill excelled. At Harrow School he won the prestigious school prize two years running. When he was fourteen he told one of his aunts: "If I had two lives I would be a soldier and a politician. But as there will be no war in my time, I will have to be a politician." His father did not think him clever enough to go to university, so he was put in the "army class" at school.

Churchill followed his father's House of Commons speeches in the newspapers, commenting on them with enthusiasm. After reading one in *The Times,* he wrote to his father: "If you will let me say so, I thought it better than anything you have done so far." The eighteen-year-old could frequently be seen listening to his father in the House of Commons, always able, because of his father's prominence, to find a place in the Distinguished Strangers' Gallery.

Not only was the parliamentary process becoming familiar to him but, on several social occasions, he met leading politicians at his parents' house. They included two future Liberal Prime Ministers, Lord Rosebery and H.H. Asquith, both of whom were impressed by his keenness and interest in the political world. On 21 April 1893, at the age of nineteen, Churchill was in the Gallery of the House of Commons when Gladstone made his masterful speech on the Second Reading of the Irish Home Rule Bill. Three decades later, Churchill was able to look at his own parliamentary work on the passage of the Irish Free State Bill as one of his most notable achievements, something Gladstone had striven for but failed to accomplish.

Edward Marjoribanks, later Viscount Tweedmouth, was Liberal Chief Whip in Gladstone's Liberal administration. In May 1893 he spent half an hour with his young nephew Churchill, describing how the Liberals could overcome the power of the House of Lords, which was refusing to vote the money needed by the Liberals for social reform. Although on that particular occasion the Conservative Peers defeated the Money Bill by 419 to 41, the battle cry "Overcoming the Peers" was to be Churchill's own cry fifteen years later, when, having left the Conservative Party, he emerged as a leading Liberal opponent of the power of the House of Lords.

While Churchill was working for his army examination, a newly elected Conservative Member of Parliament, Edward Carson, invited him to dine in the House of Commons and took him to listen to a Home Rule debate. Eighteen years later, when Carson took up Lord Randolph Churchill's slogan "Ulster will Fight, Ulster will be Right," Churchill was his leading parliamentary opponent. Churchill, as First Lord of the Admiralty, challenged Carson's paramilitary Ulster Volunteers and was willing to use the power of the Royal Navy to prevent a violent and unconstitutional attack on the British forces in Ireland.

Three weeks before his forty-sixth birthday, Lord Randolph Churchill died. Churchill was then nineteen. From that moment, although about to become a soldier and set off to distant wars, he was determined to have a parliamentary career. He wanted to fight for the policies his father had so strongly believed in: Tory Democracy and prudent government spending. After Churchill had been a cavalry officer for only two weeks, the electors of the Barnesbury constituency asked him to address them. It was his first invitation to give a political speech, but, he explained to his brother, Jack, "after much communing with myself, I wrote to them that the honour was too great—or words to that effect." Churchill declined the invitation. At the age of twenty he was already being courted by the world of politics.

In 1895 the Liberal Party was defeated at the polls, and the Conservative and Unionist Party came to power, with Lord Salisbury as Prime Minister. The Unionist section of the party was made up of former Liberals, led by Joseph Chamberlain, who had broken with Gladstone and made common cause with the Conservatives. From his army barracks, Churchill wrote to his mother: "To my mind they are too strong—too brilliant altogether. They are just the sort of Government to split on the question of Protection." Churchill could not know that when the split came a decade later, he, as young Conservative Member of Parliament, was to be a leading figure in the campaign within the party to preserve the Free Trade system and to denounce the new Prime Minister, Arthur Balfour (Lord Salisbury's nephew), for committing the party to the cause of tariffs and protective trade barriers.

While soldiering, Churchill nurtured his growing interest in politics. He was reading and rereading his father's speeches, he told his mother, "many of which I almost know by heart." His aim, he told her in 1896, shortly before his twenty-first birthday, was to win some military decorations and then "beat my sword into an iron despatch box." From India, where he travelled with his regiment, he learned that there was a parliamentary vacancy at East Bradford, the scene of one of his father's great speeches a decade earlier. "Had I been in England," he wrote to his mother, "I might have contested it and should have won." A few weeks later he wrote to her again: "What a pity I was not home for East Bradford. I see a soldier got in."

Two years of military service, "with a campaign thrown in," Churchill confided to his mother, "would I think qualify me to be allowed to beat my sword into a paper cutter & my sabretache into an election address." From India, he sent her an account of what he would include in his election address: extension of voting rights to every adult male, universal education, the establishment of all religions (not just the Church of England) and a progressive income tax. Churchill added, "I am a Liberal in all but name."

While Churchill was still in India, his mother sent him past issues of the *Annual Register of World Events,* which contained substantial extracts from parliamentary debates. As he read each volume, he annotated the debates with thoughts of his own. The method he pursued, he told his mother, was not to read any particular debate "until I have recorded my own opinion of the subject on paper, having regard only to general principles." Then, having read the debate, "I reconsider and finally write," setting out, in pencil notes that he pasted into the volumes, what he would have said in the debates had he been a Member of Parliament. His hope, he explained, was "to build up a scaffolding of logical and consistent views, which will perhaps tend to a logical and consistent mind."

In the summer of 1897, when he was twenty-two, Churchill returned to England on leave. Making his way to Conservative Party Central Office in London, he asked the party organizers to arrange a speaking engagement for him. Thus is was that on 26 June 1897 he made his first public political speech, at a Conservative rally at Claverton Manor just outside Bath. If he began, he said, with the "well worn and time-honoured apology 'unaccustomed as I am to public speaking,'" it would be "pardonable in his case" because the honour he was enjoying at that moment of "address-ing an audience of his fellow-countrymen and women was the first honour of the kind he had ever received."

Among the points Churchill made in his speech was the hope that the British worker would become a share-holder in the enterprise in which he worked, making him willing to stand the pressure of a bad year "because he shared some of the profits of a good year." As for the British Empire, Churchill wanted Britain's voice to be heard "in the councils of Europe, our sovereign sup-ported by the love of her subjects, then we shall continue to pursue that course marked out for us by an all-wise hand and carry out our mission of bearing peace, civili-sation and good government to the uttermost ends of the earth."

Churchill was already a fluent speaker, despite a life-long inability to pronounce the letter *s:* it came out as *sh.* He learned to minimize the sound, so it was hardly noticed.

———

While a soldier, Churchill saw military action on the North-West Frontier of India in 1897, in Sudan in 1898, and in South Africa in 1899 and 1900. He fought bravely and won the medals he so wished to win. But a career in the House of Common was always in his mind. His object in writing long descriptive letters about the fighting on the North-West Frontier, for publication in the *Daily Telegraph*, was, he told his mother, with the aim "of bringing my personality before the electorate" in order to give him "some political advantage."

If he were to survive the fighting, Churchill wrote to his Marlborough grandmother (Duchess Fanny), "I intend to stand for Parliament at the General Election—so that my sojourn abroad will not be indefinitely prolonged." He was still twenty-two. The next General Election was expected in 1900, fewer than three years ahead.

Even before he stood for Parliament, Churchill understood the power of oratory, writing at the time of his twenty-third birthday: "He who enjoys it wields a power more durable than that of a great king. He is an independent force in the world. Abandoned by his party, betrayed by friends, stripped of offices, whoever can command this power is still formidable." A skilful orator, Churchill added, could either "translate an established truth into simple language" or "adventurously aspire to reveal the unknown."

Churchill saw oratory as an integral part of the parliamentary system. He believed that it must inspire the listener, but it was valueless unless it also reflected the beliefs of the listener. To his brother, Churchill confided another aspect of his understanding of what would make a good parliamentarian. "A good knowledge of history," he wrote to Jack, "is a quiver full of arrows in debate."

While still in India, Churchill made a serious attempt to secure a constituency: his father's last parliamentary seat, in the London district of Paddington. As he told his mother, if she could persuade the existing Member, who was over sixty, to stand down, he would come back to England at once and enter the selection process. His mother did what she could on her son's behalf. As he later wrote of her efforts for him at that time, "She left no stone unturned, she left no cutlet uncooked." At the suggestion of Conservative Central Office, Churchill sent them an election address, should Paddington unexpectedly fall vacant, but before any election could be called the sitting member decided to stay put—and did so for another thirteen years.

Churchill was ready and eager for parliamentary life, writing to his mother: "Introductions, connections, powerful friends, a name, good advice well-followed, all these things count, but they only lead to a certain point. As it were, they may ensure admission to the scales. Ultimately every man has to be weighed, and if found wanting, nothing can procure him the public confidence." He was confident that he would not be found wanting. "I believe in myself," he told his mother. "If I did not, I might perhaps take other views."

In June 1898, aged twenty-three, Churchill returned to England once more on leave. In advance, he asked his mother to set up political meetings for him. He still had his eye on the Bradford constituency, writing to his mother that he wanted one "real, big meeting of at least 2,000 men. Compel them to come in. I am sure I can hold them. I have got lots of good material for at least three speeches, all carefully written and docketed." His mother did as he asked and, on 14 July 1898, Churchill spoke to a large crowd of Bradford working men. "I was listened to with the greatest attention for fifty-five minutes," he reported back to her, "at the end of which time there were loud and general cries of 'Go on.' Five or six times they applauded for about two minutes without stopping."

Churchill, still not at Westminster, had found the way, through preparation as well as personality, to hold and enthuse an audience. Two years later an army acquaintance wrote to him, explaining why he believed Churchill would one day be Prime Minister: "You possess the two necessary qualifications, genius and plod. Combined, I believe nothing can keep them back." These two qualities were to mark him out as a great parliamentarian, long before he became Prime Minister, and even when he was unpopular politically.

Within two weeks of his Bradford speech, Churchill was on his way to the Sudan, where he took part in the Battle of Omdurman. There he led a troop of cavalrymen and narrowly escaped death. Within two months he returned to Britain and plunged back into political speeches—and the search for a constituency. In November 1898, just before his twenty-fourth birthday, the magazine *World* stated that he was about to leave the

British Army and "come into Parliament as soon as he can." The magazine welcomed this move: "He is sure to do well; he has great ambition, great aplomb, and an unlimited amount of energy; and he has a great deal of his father's ability, besides being a good speaker." But it was to India that, as a soldier, he had to return. It was his last tour of duty.

————

Churchill left India in March 1899. Within two few weeks of his return to Britain—despite the family mourning period for his Marlborough grandmother—he had spoken at two potential constituencies, Paddington and Oldham. At a private dinner in London, two future Prime Ministers, Balfour and Asquith, were, he wrote to his mother, "markedly civil to me, I thought." They "agreed with and paid great attention to everything I said."

Six weeks after this dinner, one of the two Conservative MPs for Oldham—a two-member constituency—died unexpectedly, and Churchill was asked to stand in the by-election. Six days later he issued his election address. In his manifesto he declared himself both a Conservative and a Tory Democrat. "I regard the improvement of the condition of the British people," he wrote, "as the main end of modern government." If elected, he would promote legislation that, "without impairing the tremendous energy of production on which the wealth of our nation and the good of our people depend, may yet raise the standard of comfort and happiness in English homes." Through legislation, he would seek better conditions for the "aged poor as wide and generous as possible."

Churchill embarked with zeal on his first election campaign. "I am getting on well," he wrote to a cousin, "and scoring off all the people who ask me questions." As the campaign entered its final week, he spoke up to eight times a day. To his girlfriend, Pamela Plowden, later Countess of Lytton, he wrote: "I shall never forget the succession of great halls packed with excited people until there was not room for one single person more—speech after speech—meeting after meeting—three even four in one night—intermittent flashes of Heat & Light & enthusiasm—with cold air and the rattle of a carriage in between." He was also pleased to report to her: "I have hardly repeated myself at all. And at each meeting I am conscious of growing powers—and facilities of speech."

Churchill was unsuccessful. He and his fellow Conservative candidate were defeated by the two Liberal candidates by narrow margins. Churchill lost by only 1,500 votes out of 24,300. His efforts were watched with approval at the highest level. "Winston made a splendid fight," the Prime Minister, Lord Salisbury, wrote to Churchill's mother. Asquith, a future Liberal Prime Minister in whose Cabinet Churchill would serve, wrote to her: "Winston's good fight at Oldham gives him his spurs." Churchill wrote to a friend: "I speak now quite easily without preparation, which is a new weapon that will not wear out."

Three months after his failure to be elected to Parliament, Churchill left Britain for South Africa as a war correspondent. Two days before embarking on the journey there, by ship from Southampton, he went to Oldham, where, at a public meeting, he promised to come back and win the seat at the General Election—whenever that might be.

————

Two weeks after reaching South Africa, while travelling as a journalist on a British military armoured train, Churchill was captured by the Boers. After a month as a prisoner of war, he escaped and made his way back to British-held territory. Reaching Durban at a time of continual British setbacks on the battlefield, he found that his escape had made him a popular hero, celebrated in songs and cartoons. He rejoined the army and returned to the battlefield, both to fight and to continue as a war correspondent, sending regular dispatches to the *Morning Post* in London. "Ah, horrible war," he wrote in a war report in mid-January 1900, "amazing medley of the glorious and squalid, the pitiful and the sublime; if modern men of light and leading saw your face closer, simple folk would see it hardly ever."

Churchill fought bravely in a dozen battles. When he received a request from the Conservative electors of Southport—a Lancashire constituency—to be their candidate at the next General Election, he declined. He wanted to see the war to a conclusion. But his thoughts never strayed far from the parliamentary battles that lay ahead. After describing the relief of the siege of Ladysmith, he wrote of his conviction that, once the war was won, "the people of England must devote themselves to stimulating and sustaining the spirit of the people by measures of social improvement and reform."

Churchill remained in South Africa, mainly in the fighting line, until the summer of 1900. While he was in action, several constituencies asked him to stand for them at the next General Election. Oldham was among the supplicants. "They have implored me not to desert them," he explained to his mother, nor did he. On 7 July 1900 Churchill left South Africa. While he was on the ship returning to Britain, a sketch writer in *Vanity Fair* wrote that the returning soldier had "hankered after politics since he was a small boy, and it is probable that his every effort, military or literary, has been made with political bent." The writer went on to say with prescience, "he can hardly be the slave of any Party."

2

The Parliamentary Arena

The essence of parliamentary democracy is the range of political opinions that seek to work within an electoral and democratic framework. Churchill was to understand and accept that mix from the outset of his parliamentary career. That career began with an upsurge of activity and acceptance. Five days after his ship docked at Southampton, he went to Oldham, where he was adopted as the prospective Conservative candidate. Returning to London, a member of the Conservative Government invited him to the House of Commons, where he was entertained on the terrace "and all sorts of members," including Joseph Chamberlain, "came up and generally gave me a very flattering reception."

Campaigning at Oldham began on 19 November 1900. In an election where polling was spread over three weeks, the Oldham result was one of the first to be announced. In an exceptionally close result, in which his fellow Conservative challenger was defeated, Churchill was elected. On the eve of his twenty-sixth birthday, his parliamentary career had begun.

Before Churchill could return to London, Arthur Balfour, the Conservative leader and Lord Salisbury's successor as Prime Minister, asked him to help out in constituencies that had not yet polled, including Balfour's own. "No man who ever got into Parliament," St. John Brodrick, the new Secretary of State for War, wrote to Churchill, "has done more than you have done in the last two years to enable him to represent a constituency." His "only regret," Brodrick added—with what was to prove unerring perspicacity—" is that to all appearances you will now be in Opposition, for your artillery will inevitably be directed against us!"

As Brodrick had forecast, during Churchill's first four years in Parliament, the Member for Oldham not only made repeated contributions to the debates but also fearlessly criticized his own party Members whenever he felt—as he often did—that they were misguided. The ability, indeed the duty, of Members of Parliament to express independent views was a central theme of Churchill's concept of parliamentary democracy. It did not sit well with the party managers—the Whips of both parties for which, in different decades, he was to take his seat—who tried, as was their duty, to turn him into a compliant party member.

During his first four years at Westminster, Churchill learned every skill and pitfall of the parliamentarian's art. He first took his seat, on the Conservative benches, on 14 February 1901. Two weeks later, in his maiden speech, he criticized the attitude, prevalent in Conservative circles, of hostility to the British adversary in South Africa. "If I were a Boer," he said, "I hope I should be fighting in the field," and he went on to express his views of war—views that he was to hold throughout his life—which were not to the taste of many of his Conservative listeners in the Chamber. If there were those who "rejoiced in this war," he said, "and went out with hopes of excitement or the lust of conflict, they have had enough, and more than enough, today."

Parliamentary democracy depends on the quality and range of parliamentary debate. Churchill was seen at once to meet the highest standards, as the *Daily Telegraph* parliamentary correspondent wrote of him: "Perfectly at home, with lively gestures that pointed his sparkling sentences, he instantly caught the tone and ear of the House crowded in every part."

Two weeks after his maiden speech, Churchill was warning his own party leaders, even when defending them against the demand for an inquiry into the dismissal of a general in South Africa: "I have noticed in the last three wars in which we have been engaged a tendency—arising partly from good nature towards their comrades, partly from dislike of public scrutiny—to hush everything up, to make everything look as fair as possible, to tell the official truth, to present a version of the truth which contains about seventy-five percent of the actual article." From Lord Curzon, the Viceroy of India, and a friend of

Churchill's mother, came wise advice: "There is no more difficult position than being on the benches behind a Government. It is hard to strike the mean between independence & loyalty. The great thing is to impress the House with earnestness. They will forgive anything but flippancy."

There was nothing flippant in Churchill's sustained attack in the coming months, during several debates, on his own Government's proposed increase in military expenditure. The chief target of his criticisms was the Secretary of State for War, St. John Brodrick. It was Churchill himself who tabled an amendment to Brodrick's army scheme. On 13 May 1900, fewer than three months after his maiden speech, Churchill set out his criticisms in a speech of considerable power, skill and courage, a forerunner of speeches that he was to make, year in and year out, during more than half a century at Westminster. It was the cause of excessive government expenditure—the cause for which his father had resigned as Chancellor of the Exchequer in 1886—that Churchill put forward. He was "very glad," he said, "that the House has allowed me, after an interval of fifteen years, to lift again the tattered flag of retrenchment and economy."

Four months after taking his place on the Conservative benches, Churchill had become a dissident Conservative, opposed to what he regarded as their excessive spending plans for the army. His attack on what he called "Mr.

Brodrick's Army"—the title he gave to a pamphlet of his collected speeches on the topic—was sustained and uncompromising. "I have frequently been astonished," he said in his speech of May 13, "with what composure and how glibly Members, and even Ministers, talk of a European war," and he went on to warn that such a war "can only end in the ruin of the vanquished and the scarcely less fatal commercial dislocation and exhaustion of the conquerors . . . We do not know what war is. We have had a glimpse of it in South Africa. Even in minia-ture it is hideous and appalling."

That summer Churchill joined forces with a number of other young Conservative Members of Parliament who were uneasy with their leaders' policies. Every Thursday when Parliament was in session, they dined together in the House, inviting as their guest a senior politician with whom they could express their unease and discuss their ideas for reform. Among their guests was a former Liberal Prime Minister, Lord Rosebery. Churchill was also invited to dine with two leading Liberal Members of the parliamentary opposition—Asquith, and Sir Edward Grey, later the Foreign Secretary.

———

Churchill's first serious breach with his party leaders came over the conduct of the Boer War. Even as the war was drawing to a close, Churchill protested publicly against the execution of a Boer commandant by the British military authorities in South Africa. He wanted to see reconciliation between "Boer and Briton," not, as he told an audience at Saddleworth, in Yorkshire, in October 1901, a growing "gulf of hatred." (In 1945 he was to say of the Germans: "My hate ended with their surrender.")

During his speech at Saddleworth, Churchill raised one of the central issues of parliamentary democracy— the wide-ranging responsibilities of the Government party in the House of Commons. It was wrong, he insisted, for the Conservative leaders—his own leaders, the Prime Minister Arthur Balfour and the Colonial Secretary Joseph Chamberlain—to say that responsibility for the execution of the Boer commandant was not theirs but that of the local military authorities. "I warn these two distinguished gentlemen," he declared, "that they cannot devolve upon others the weight and burden of the war." To Chamberlain he wrote directly: "Nothing can relieve the Government of their responsibility."

Churchill wanted Parliament to move forward with wide-ranging measures of social reform—measures that were far more attractive to the Liberal Opposition than to his own Conservative leaders. In mid-December 1901, two weeks after his twenty-seventh birthday and less than a year since he had entered Parliament, Churchill dined with John Morley, a leading Liberal reformer. Morley recommended to Churchill that he read Seebohm

Rowntree's study of poverty in the city of York. Churchill was so struck by the book's account of inequality that he set down his own reflections on it in writing. In his notes he stressed the need for Government to address the questions of poverty, unemployment and inadequate housing: "This festering life at home makes worldwide power a mockery." It was "a terrible thing," he told a Conservative meeting in Blackpool, that there were people, such as those in York, "who have . . . the workhouse or prison as the only avenues to change from their present situation."

On 24 April 1902, Churchill raised this issue of urban poverty in Parliament, asking Balfour to appoint a Select Committee of the House "to report and consider whether national expenditure cannot be diminished without injury to the public service, and whether the money voted cannot be apportioned to better advantage than at present." After some hesitation, Balfour agreed to a Select Committee and appointed Churchill one of its members, but the Conservative Party had no interest in promoting social reform on the scale Churchill believed essential.

Churchill believed that these social issues must be fought in civilized debate in the House of Commons, and not in violence at political meetings. When Conservative supporters in Birmingham turned in fury against the rising Liberal politician David Lloyd George, threatening him physically, Churchill was outraged. As far as he was concerned, he wrote in a private letter to a friend,

Lloyd George was a "chattering little cad," but every man had a "perfect right" to express his opinions, To shout down opinions "because they are odious to the majority in the district is a very dangerous, fatal doctrine for the Conservative Party."

More and more, Churchill was attracted by what he called "the Government of the Middle." He was writing his father's biography and felt strongly that such a government was one his father would have liked to have led: a party of the middle that could appeal to those who found nothing helpful or edifying in the harsh antics of Conservative-Liberal confrontation. In the biography, Churchill wrote of an England "of wise men who gaze without self-deception at the failures and follies of both political parties; of brave and earnest men who find in neither faction fair scope for the effort that is in them; of 'poor men' who increasingly doubt the sincerity of party philosophy."

In a letter to a senior member of the Conservative Party organization at Oldham, Churchill explained his hopes for "the gradual creation by an evolutionary process of a Democratic or Progressive wing to the Conservative Party, which could either join a central coalition or infuse vitality into the parent body."

To the former Liberal Prime Minister, Lord Rosebery, Churchill set out his thoughts on the Government of the Middle in a letter on 10 October 1902. Such a government, he wrote, "shall be free at once from the sordid selfishness & callousness of Toryism on the one hand & the blind appetites of the radical masses on the other." The "one difficulty" he had in putting this idea forward, Churchill conceded, "is the suspicion that I am moved by mere restless ambition." If some "definite issue—such as tariff—were to arise—that difficulty would disappear." Churchill was a convinced Free Trader, opposed to all forms of protective tariffs.

Churchill's first vote against his own party came on 1 February 1903, when he spoke against the Government's continuing search for increased military expenditure. He was one of eighteen Conservatives to defy the party Whip and vote with the Liberal Opposition. "I think it is the most successful speech I have yet made," he wrote to Rosebery, "and the House of Commons purred like an amiable cat." That purring came primarily from the Liberal Opposition benches.

Reflecting on the considerable frustrations of wanting to pursue policies that were rejected by the parliamentary majority, Churchill wrote to the Leader of the Liberal Party, Sir Henry Campbell-Bannerman, in a letter that expressed his anxieties about the party system: "It is of course utterly impossible for any private member acting alone to influence in the slightest degree the policy of a powerful government. He may make speeches; but that is all. Hardly any question is ever decided on its merits. Divisions are taken on strict Party lines and Ministers have at their disposal a monopoly of expert opinion for and against every conceivable course, a battalion of drilled supporters, and the last word in all debates." Twenty-five years later the tyranny of the party machine was to be Churchill's charge against Neville Chamberlain (Joseph Chamberlain's son) and his ministerial colleagues in the appeasement debates, as it had been against Ramsay MacDonald and Stanley Baldwin throughout the 1930s.

On 24 May 1903 Churchill wrote to a constituent that what he had in mind was "that grand ideal of a National party of which Lord Randolph dreamed and for which he toiled." Three weeks later, on 15 May 1903, a fateful day for British politics and a decisive day in Churchill's career, the Unionist leader Joseph Chamberlain—the twin pillar with Balfour of Conservative political power—raised the banner of Tariff Reform. Speaking in Birmingham, Chamberlain called for an end to Free Trade and the creation of protective tariffs for British and Colonial industry. Colonial goods would be allowed into Britain without a tax. European goods would be taxed, to protect the British producers.

Churchill had found the issue on which he would challenge the whole Conservative Party machine. It was he who, at the age of twenty-eight, answered Chamberlain five days later, on May 20, in a speech in Hoxton. It was a struggle for the soul of the Conservative Party. "I am utterly opposed," he wrote to Balfour, "to anything which will alter the Free Trade character of this country."

Speeches outside Parliament were an important aspect of parliamentary democracy—taking the arguments to the people. But at its core was Parliament itself, the Chamber of the House of Commons. On May 28, eight days after his Hoxton speech, Churchill listened in the Chamber as Chamberlain set out the case for Protection. No one on the Liberal benches rose to answer him. Churchill therefore rose himself: an astonishing act by a backbench Member of Parliament against one of his own leaders, a giant on the parliamentary scene. If Protection were to become Conservative policy, Churchill warned, "the old Conservative Party, with its religious convictions and constitutional principles, will disappear, and a new Party will arise, rich, materialistic and secular, whose opinions will turn on tariffs and who will cause the lobbies to be crowded with the touts of protected industries."

Determined to preserve Free Trade, Churchill was helped in establishing a Free Food League by a dozen like-minded younger Conservative Members of Parliament—also in their twenties and thirties—who were committed to retaining the Free Trade aspect of Conservatism and who rejected protecting British goods by means of tariff barriers. They threatened to stand against the party at the next General Election and to give their support to the Liberals, if the Conservative Party became the standard-bearer for tariffs. When the League was launched on 13 July 1903, sixty Conservative MPs joined it. They called themselves Unionist Free Traders, a new political grouping in the House of Commons. "Let me say in strictest confidence," Churchill wrote to one of them, "that my idea is, and has always been, some sort of central government being formed."

No such central government came into being. Balfour, after much hesitation—acerbically exploited by Churchill in the House of Commons—committed the Conservative Party to tariffs. Within a few days the Liberal Association of Birmingham Central—where Lord Randolph had once fought—invited Churchill to be its candidate at the next election. He declined, still hoping that the Unionist Free Traders could form an independent parliamentary grouping. To his chagrin, the Liberal leadership refused a suggestion that, in the coming election, the Unionist Free Trade candidates— of which he would be one—would not have Liberal candidates put up against them. The Liberal Party machine, Churchill wrote to a friend in despair, "seems to be just as stupid and brutalised as ours."

More offers to stand for Parliament as a Liberal reached Churchill at the end of 1903. His Liberal uncle, Lord Tweedmouth, asked if he would like to stand for the Scottish constituency of Sutherland. He declined, but he did send a message of support to the Liberal candidate in a by-election in another constituency, Ludlow. A few days later, in a speech in Halifax, Churchill angered his Unionist Free Trader colleagues still further when he declared, "Thank God we have an Opposition."

Churchill effectively joined that Opposition on 2 May 1904, when he spoke in Parliament against the Conservative decision to give West Indian sugar a protected price against all non-Colonial markets. He took the opportunity of his speech to put forward his thoughts on the unfairness of a parliamentary system where vested interests dominated the political structure. "It was always found in the past," he said, "to be a misfortune to a country when it was governed from one particular point of view, or in the interests of any particular class, whether it was the Court or the Church, or the Army or the mercantile or labouring classes. Every country ought to be governed from some central point of view, where all classes and all interests are proportionately represented."

In March 1904 Churchill supported a Liberal vote of censure against the Government's use of indentured Chinese labour in South Africa, arguing that it was the duty of the Westminster Parliament to be concerned with the plight of all those who were ill-treated anywhere in the British Empire. He also voted in favour of Liberal bills to restore legal rights to the trade unions and to tax the sale of land when it was bought cheaply and then sold at a far higher price as building land. (This legislation, which Churchill was to advocate again in 1918, only entered the Statute Book fifty-five years later, in 1969, in Harold Wilson's premiership.)

On 18 April 1904 Churchill accepted an invitation from the Liberals of North-West Manchester to stand as a Free Trade candidate, with full Liberal support. He accepted. Six weeks later, in Manchester, he publicly denounced the Government's Aliens Bill, aimed to curb foreign—and largely Jewish—immigration. His attack was published in the newspapers on May 31. It was the first parliamentary day after the Whitsun recess. That day Churchill took the step that was to alienate him for many years from a sizable portion of the Conservative Party. He entered the Chamber of the House of Commons, stood for a moment at the Bar of the House, looked briefly at the Government benches to his left and the Opposition benches to his right, walked up the aisle, bowed to the Speaker, turned sharply and emphatically to his right, and took his seat on the Liberal benches.

"Crossing the floor of the House," as it is called, was Churchill's ultimate assertion of the freedom of an individual Member of Parliament within the parliamentary system. The seat he chose was that in which his father had sat during his years in Opposition. On the Liberal benches he became the scourge of his former Conservative colleagues—not that he had given them much peace when he was one of their number. When the Government introduced its Aliens Bill, Churchill challenged it clause by clause on the floor of the House. At Carnarvon he shared a platform with one of the Liberal Party's most radical members, David Lloyd George. At Edinburgh he declared that he was more afraid of the "Independent Capitalist Party" than the Independent

Labour Party, a Labour left-wing grouping. Churchill had always been an opponent of monopoly capitalism. Capitalism "in the form of Trusts," he had written to an American friend five years earlier, "has reached a pitch of power which the old economists never contemplated and which excites my most lively terror."

3

The Challenge of Legislation

Among the tests of the effectiveness and value of parliamentary democracy is the quality of the legislation passed by Parliament. An opportunity arose before Churchill had been in the House of Commons for five years whereby he would be tested in this demanding sphere. On 4 December 1904, feeling that the Liberal Party was in disarray and would lose a General Election, Arthur Balfour resigned as Prime Minister and his Conservative administration came to an end. King Edward VII asked the Liberal leader, Sir Henry Campbell-Bannerman, to form a Government. Churchill, the newcomer to the Liberal benches, was appointed to the junior ministerial position of Under-Secretary of State for the Colonies.

Churchill's entry into the Government came a week after his thirty-first birthday. His ministerial and legislative career had begun, as he plunged, for the first time, into the responsibilities of a parliamentarian in Government office. Henceforth the demands of ministerial office, some extremely onerous, were to be his in every decade during a turbulent half century.

In those first years of ministerial responsibility in the House of Commons, in an assertion of the values of parliamentary democracy, Churchill asserted the rights of Black subjects of the British Empire to the concern and protection of the Westminster Parliament: "Our responsibilities to the native races remains a real one," he told a correspondent.

In the legislation that he piloted through the House of Commons to secure peace in South Africa, he urged "a message of tolerance and conciliation to warring races" of Briton and Boer. "Do not let us do anything," he wrote to the Cabinet, "which makes us the champions of one race and deprives us forever of the confidence of the other." In a sustained effort involving the answering of some five hundred parliamentary questions, he piloted the Orange Free State and Transvaal Constitution bills through Parliament, clause by clause.

A capacity for hard work was one of Churchill's great strengths: "Work, which is a joy," he once called it. Parliamentary democracy could not be sustained by opposition and oratory alone. He would sometimes quote a verse that could well have been his motto:

The heights achieved by men and kept
Were not achieved by sudden flight
But they, while their companions slept
Were toiling upwards through the night.

Another quotation, Talleyrand's description of Napoleon, could also apply to Churchill: he possessed "the art of fixing his mind upon a topic for a long period of time without becoming tired" (L'art de fixer sur un object longtemps sans être fatigué). This diligence certainly was true of Churchill's administrative and legislative efforts between 1906 and 1911, a high point of his active assertion of parliamentary democracy. "Our duty," he wrote to Lord Elgin, his Colonial Office chief, "is to insist that the principles of justice and the safeguards of judicial procedures are rigidly, punctiliously and pedantically followed." When the Governor of Ceylon pleaded "inconvenience" as a reason for not following up a case of alleged injustice, Churchill wrote to Elgin: "The inconvenience inseparable from the reparation of injustice or irregularity is one of the safeguards against their recurrence." When a Zulu revolt in Natal was crushed with severity, Churchill protested to Elgin about the "disgusting butchery."

A Junior Minister could not change the ethos of the Colonial civil service, but he could try to change the direction of parliamentary concerns at home. In a speech in Glasgow on 11 October 1906, he set out a panorama of measures whereby Parliament could strike out through legislation against inequalities in the nature of British society. The time had come, he asserted, for State intervention across the whole social field. The State, he said, must "increasingly and earnestly concern itself with the care of the sick and aged, and, above all, of the children." The State should take a lead in replanting the forests that had been denuded of trees by those in search of profitable timber. The State should also assume the position "of the reserve employer of labour." Above all, Churchill said, "I look forward to the universal establishment of minimum standards of life and labour, and their progressive elevation. . . . We want to draw a line below which we will not allow persons to live and labour, yet above which they may compete with all the strength of their manhood. We want to have free competition upwards; we decline to allow free competition to run downwards. We do not want to pull down the structure of science and civilisation, but to spread a net over the abyss."

From these words came pioneering legislation. Appointed in 1908 to the Cabinet as President of the Board of Trade, after H.H. Asquith had succeeded the ailing Campbell-Bannerman as Prime Minister, Churchill drafted, introduced and piloted through Parliament a series of Bills that took their place on the Statute Book of progressive legislation. The Mines Eight Hours Act reduced the hours of work underground from eight to six. In other acts and measures that he introduced, Government shipbuilding orders were transferred to dockyards where there was high unemployment. More than two hundred Labour Exchanges nationwide, an innovation of Churchill's inventive mind, enabled the unemployed in one part of the country to find work elsewhere. A senior Labour Member of Parliament, Arthur Henderson—the Labour Party was then emerging as a political force—called Churchill's announcement of Labour Exchanges "one of the most far-reaching statements which has been delivered during the time I have been associated with Parliament."

Another piece of legislation that Churchill piloted through Parliament was the Trades Boards Act. This law was a major blow at the widespread system of sweated labour. It established inspectors who had the powers to prosecute any employer who was exploiting his workers, either by exceptionally low wages or by "conditions prejudicial to physical and social welfare." A Standing Court of Arbitration put the arbitration of industrial disputes on an impartial plane, with employers and employees equally represented: in its first twelve months, the Court settled seven major industrial disputes.

On becoming President of the Board of Trade in 1908, Churchill had, according to the rules of the time, to seek re-election. He was defeated in his Manchester constituency but found a seat at Dundee. That same year, as well as a Scottish constituency, he found a Scottish wife—Clementine. She much approved of his parliamentary reforming zeal, which, after the end of the First World War, she was to urge him to resume.

The climax of Churchill's social reform measures as President of the Board of Trade was a comprehensive scheme for national unemployment insurance: the employer, the employee and the State would each contribute. This scheme, on which Churchill worked with enormous energy and enthusiasm, created the system of national insurance that has lasted until this day as a basic feature of social equity and prudence. In its first phase, three million working men, mostly in shipbuilding and engineering, were to be its beneficiaries.

Churchill introduced the scheme to the Cabinet, which accepted it. Unfortunately for him, he left the Board of Trade before his scheme could be introduced to Parliament: it was Lloyd George who introduced it and took the credit. "Lloyd George has practically taken unemployment insurance to his own bosom," Churchill wrote to Clementine in the spring of 1911, "& I am I think effectively elbowed out of this large field in which I consumed so much thought & effort. Never mind! There are a good many fish in the sea."

————

In August 1909 the overwhelming Conservative majority in the House of Lords announced that it would use its existing veto powers to turn down Lloyd George's forthcoming budget. The House of Lords had the power to reject all Money Bills—proposals coming from the House of Commons which involved expenditure. The use of this veto power would make it impossible for the budget—containing many measures Churchill had either initiated or approved—to pass.

To preserve the budget intact, the Liberals began a campaign against the veto power of the House of Lords. Churchill was at the forefront of that campaign. He had already, in the House of Commons two years earlier, on 29 June 1907, described the House of Lords as "one-sided, hereditary, unpurged, unrepresented, irresponsible, absentee." In a speech at Leicester on 6 September 1909, Churchill warned of the dangers if the budget proposals were rejected. "If we carry on in the old happy-go-lucky way," he said, "the richer classes ever growing in wealth and number, the very poor remaining plunged or plunging ever deeper into helpless, hopeless misery, then I think there is nothing before us but the savage strife between class and class, and an increasing disorganisation, with the increasing loss of human strength and happiness."

On 30 November 1909, Churchill's thirty-fifth birthday, the House of Lords rejected the budget by 350 votes to 75. Four days later, Asquith called a General Election. The Liberal election cry, which Churchill echoed as loudly as anyone, declared "The Peers versus the People." Throughout the election campaign, Churchill was at the forefront of the attack on the Money Bill veto powers of the Lords. The Liberals won the election, but only just. The Irish Nationalists, who won 84 seats, held the balance of power, with

Liberals and Conservatives almost equally balanced, 275 to 272. Labour won 42 seats.

Following the election, Churchill was sent by Asquith to the Home Office. It fell to him, as Home Secretary, to introduce in the Commons the measures to curb the powers of the House of Lords. His speech of 31 March 1910 was a highpoint of parliamentary advocacy. It was necessary, he said, for the "Crown and Commons," acting together, to "restore the balance of the Constitution and restrict for ever the Veto of the House of Lords." Within a year, the Parliament Act of 1911 was to end for all time the Money Bill veto powers of the Lords.

Churchill believed that the House of Commons had the right to know, and to accept, the principles that lay behind actions by the executive. During unrest at Tonypandy, a coal-mining town in South Wales, the War Office sent armed soldiers from London to restore order. As soon as he was told, Churchill ordered the troop train to be halted, and the troops returned to London. In their place he sent London policemen—unarmed. In the House of Commons the Conservatives denounced him for softness and timidity. He defended his recall of the troops when he spoke in the House of Commons: "It must be the object of public policy," he said, "to avoid collisions between troops and people engaged in industrial disputes." The Conservatives rejected this principle; the Liberals, with their tiny majority, accepted it. Churchill's action, commented the

Manchester Guardian, "in all probability saved many lives." Yet, in a cruel irony of history, Churchill was to be accused by generations of Labour politicians (among them a future Leader of the Labour Party, Neil Kinnock) of using troops at Tonypandy.

Churchill continued to be at the forefront of social legislation. His Coal Mines Act created stricter safety standards, sought to eliminate cruelty to pit ponies, and instituted pithead baths for the miners. His Shops Act created one early closing day a week and compulsory intervals for shop assistants' meals. Other proposals in the Bill, including a reduction of regular hours of work from eighty to sixty a week and the strict regulation of overtime (for which Churchill had fought), were rejected by the House. Nine years were to elapse before they, too, were put on the Statute Book.

Churchill took a particularly strong line in Parliament against judges who, he declared, were acting unfairly against the Trade Unions. It was his intention, he told the House, "to relieve Trade Unions from the harassing litigation to which they have been exposed and set them free to develop their work without the perpetual check and uncertainty of frequent interruption, and without being brought constantly into contact with the courts." For Churchill—whose attitude was denounced by the Conservatives as "deeply deplorable" and "mischievous"—judges could not be allowed to avoid the scrutiny of Parliament.

It was the breadth of his prison reforms that most impressed Churchill's parliamentary colleagues. He persuaded the House of Commons to reduce drastically the number of people in prison, to curtail the time spent in solitary confinement, and to abolish automatic imprisonment for non-payment of fines—a rule whereby many suffragettes had been sent to prison. Within five years of Churchill's new rule, the number of those imprisoned for short periods or for being unable or unwilling to pay their fines (many of which were for drunkenness) dropped from 62,000 to 5,000. The number of young offenders being sent to Borstal was likewise reduced. An upper limit in sentencing was created for specific offences, and, for the first time, libraries were established in prison, and lectures and concerts arranged.

Also for the first time, as a result of Churchill's reforms, a distinction was made in the treatment of criminal and political prisoners. Prison rules, Churchill told the House of Commons, which were "suitable for criminals jailed for dishonesty or cruelty or other crimes implying moral turpitude, should not be applied inflexibly to those whose general character is good and whose offences, however reprehensible, do not involve personal dishonour."

When Churchill became Home Secretary in 1910, more than 12,000 boys between the ages of sixteen and twenty were in prisons. Churchill introduced new rules whereby that number dropped to below 2,000. He explained all this to the House of Commons in patient detail, with graphic illustrations, as befitted someone who had himself been a prisoner. Some of Churchill's would-be reforms, too liberal for the Liberal Government, had to wait almost forty years, until Clement Attlee's Labour Government passed its Criminal Justice Act in 1948.

One particular achievement was Churchill's abolition of police supervision of released convicts. He replaced this practice with a central agency for the care of prisoners after their release. It was no longer to be the police, but representatives of the existing Prisoners' Aid Societies, who would monitor prisoners after release. Police supervision, Churchill explained to the House, failed altogether "to enable or encourage a convict to resume his place in honest industry. A supervision more individualised, more intimate, more carefully considered, more philanthropically inspired, is necessary." The Probation Service was born—through Churchill's imaginative humanity and the parliamentary process.

Churchill saw a role for parliamentary democracy even with regard to convicted criminals. On 10 July 1910, he urged the House of Commons to accept "a calm and dispassionate recognition of the rights of the accused against the State, and even of convicted criminals against the State, a constant heart-searching by all charged with the duty of punishment, a desire and eagerness to rehabilitate in the world of industry all those who have paid their dues in the hard coinage of punishment, tireless efforts towards the discovery of curative and regenerating processes, and an unfaltering faith that there is a treasure, if only you can find it, in the heart of every man." These qualities, Churchill added, "are the symbols which in the treatment of crime and criminals mark and measure the stored-up strength of a nation, and are the sign and proof of the living virtue in it." Fifty-three years later, Robert Kennedy, then Attorney-General of the United States, asked me to read Churchill's words to him over the telephone. He later wrote of the impact they had made on him as he grappled with his own criminal justice legislation.

Churchill also told the House of Commons: "We must not forget that when every material improvement has been effected in prisons, when the temperature has been adjusted, when the proper food to maintain health and strength has been given, when the doctors, chaplains and prison visitors have come and gone, the convict stands deprived of everything that a free man calls life. We must not forget that all these improvements, which are sometimes slaves to our consciences, do not change that position."

———

Once again, the question of Ireland's political future threatened to disrupt and even destroy the British parliamentary system—as it had done in 1893 when the young Churchill watched as Gladstone introduced his Home Rule Bill. In the second General Election of 1910, held in December, the result of which was almost identical to the first, the Irish Nationalists, with 86 seats, held the balance of power. Liberals and Conservatives were almost equally balanced, 272 against 270. Labour won 44 seats. Given the Irish parliamentary stranglehold, the Liberal Government had to go ahead with Home Rule legislation. But the Conservative opposition, within a few votes of equality on the floor of the House, had the power to disrupt government business.

As the Irish crisis intensified and the Parliament Act of 1911 stripped away the Money Bill veto of the House of Lords, an intensification of political passions arose that threatened the very fabric of parliamentary democracy. Irish, Liberal and Conservative factions spoke in the language of growing extremism and violence. An essential part of Churchill's concept of parliamentary democracy was his belief that nothing, even in the bitterest political controversy, must be allowed to damage the fabric of peaceful debate and civilized discourse. It was his strong conviction that, within the democratic system, all political disagreements, whether within a party or between parties, must not involve personal animosities. If allowed to fester, he believed, such animosities would endanger the democratic process. For this reason, at the height of the political controversies of 1911, he became one of the founders of a new political club, the Other Club.

The Other Club was an attempt to bring together Liberal and Tory leaders, and non-political figures of stature, in fortnightly social gatherings that would bridge the political gulfs and quarrels of the day. "Great tact will be necessary," Churchill explained to the Conservative leader, Andrew Bonar Law, "in the avoidance of bad moments." The Other Club met for dinner at the Savoy Hotel once every two weeks while Parliament was in session, holding its first dinner on 18 May 1911. A few weeks earlier, Churchill had been hit on the head by a book thrown by a Conservative MP opposed to Irish Home Rule, drawing blood. Politicians who might have come to blows in the House of Commons found at the Other Club the calm and conviviality that enabled them to maintain and preserve the essential civilities of parliamentary discourse.

As a parliamentarian, Churchill put great store in the power of argument. For every few minutes of oratory, he would present half an hour or more of detailed, patient explanation. As First Lord of the Admiralty after October 1911, he had to present complex facts and figures, projections and comparisons. During the Navy Estimates debate on 22 July 1912 he spoke for more than two hours on the new German Navy Law and Britain's required firm response. On 28 April 1914, at the height of the Ulster confrontation, as civil war loomed, he put forward with patience and intricate argument a compromise designed to safeguard Ulster's interests without denying predominantly Catholic Ireland the benefits of Home Rule.

After the second General Election in 1910, Churchill suggested to Asquith a compromise with the Conservatives so that the two parties could work together on a common social and imperial policy. During the Parliament Bill debates in 1911, Asquith—at times too affected by drink to conduct the behind-the-scenes evening negotiations with Balfour—entrusted them to Churchill. When the Parliament Act had been passed, Churchill wrote to the new King, George V, that it was to be hoped "that a period of co-operation between the two branches of the legislature may now set in & that the settlement of several out of date quarrels may lead to a truer sense of national unity."

Churchill was again at the centre of a search for compromise in the early months of 1914, as negotiations took place in London between the Irish Nationalists, determined on Home Rule, and the Ulster Conservatives, equally determined not to allow any political power to be transferred from Westminster to Dublin. Churchill was in the Cabinet room during urgent talks on the latest border proposals between Ulster and the rest of Ireland when the discussion was brought to a somewhat abrupt and unexpected end by Sir Edward Grey, who reported that the Archduke Franz Ferdinand of Austria had been assassinated in Sarajevo.

As war clouds loomed, Churchill put forward the idea of a Liberal-Conservative coalition, to ensure that the war crisis was met with unity and determination across the political divide. Several senior Conservatives supported the idea, but the party Leader, Andrew Bonar Law, did not.

4

The Parliamentary Scene in
War and Reconstruction

When war came in August 1914, Britain had not
been at war in continental Europe for almost a
hundred years, since the defeat of Napoleon at the
Battle of Waterloo in 1815. The First World War was
the first to be fought with a parliamentary system based
on universal manhood suffrage (women did not yet have
the vote in Britain). At the outbreak of war, Churchill
had been First Lord of the Admiralty for nearly three
years. His new wartime responsibilities, for which he
was ultimately responsible to Parliament, included
ensuring the safe passage of the British Expeditionary
Force to France, supervising the aerial defence of
Britain, and meeting and countering German naval
attacks on British merchant shipping. He also
embarked on a naval expedition against the Ottoman
Empire at the Dardanelles, hoping thereby to shorten
the war by striking at the weakest of the Central
Powers. When the naval attack failed, the Secretary of
State for War, Lord Kitchener, decided to launch a military landing at the Gallipoli Peninsula.

Even while the battle was being fought at Gallipoli, and long before its outcome was certain, the Prime Minister H. H. Asquith was forced by the Conservatives, largely as a result of a severe shell shortage on the Western Front, to form a coalition government. The Conservatives had one condition for joining: that Churchill leave the Admiralty. His attacks on them in Parliament during the previous decade, particularly over their hostility to Irish Home Rule, was more than they would tolerate. He left the Admiralty in May 1915 and was given a sinecure position as Chancellor of the Duchy of Lancaster, still a member of the inner cabinet but with no ministerial responsibilities. In November, frustrated at having no influence over war policy, he left the Government altogether.

Calling himself the "escaped scapegoat," Churchill went to the Western Front, where he commanded an infantry battalion for six months and faced the uncertainty and perils of front-line service under enemy fire. He returned only once to Britain, in March 1916, to raise in Parliament what he regarded as the Admiralty's failures in the war at sea. (Balfour had replaced him as First Lord of the Admiralty.)

In May 1916 Churchill's battalion was amalgamated with another. He returned to his parliamentary duties, pleading in the House of Commons for an understanding of the unfair burdens put on the men in the trenches. In one speech he pointed out that the majority of soldiers serving in France—working in the lines of communication—never went near the front. It was, he said, "one of the grimmest class distinctions ever drawn in this world": the separation of soldiers into the fighting men and those who provided services for them in the security of the ports and approach roads.

Churchill wanted the House to realize the harshness of front-line service: "I say to myself every day, what is going on while we sit here, while we go away to dinner or home to bed? Nearly a thousand men—Englishmen, Britishers, men of our race—are knocked into bundles of bloody rags every twenty-four hours, and carried away to hasty graves or to field ambulances." It was six weeks before the opening of the Somme offensive. Churchill spoke in Parliament against the "futile offensives," but his voice was drowned in the general patriotic call for more and more attacks against the virtually impregnable German line.

On a personal note, Churchill begged Asquith to allow Parliament to see all the documents he had assembled to give the true story of the naval attack on the Dardanelles. Asquith refused. When Lloyd George succeeded Asquith as Prime Minister in December 1916, the ban remained in force. Churchill had faith in the fairness of Parliament but was not allowed to put that faith to the test. He was never allowed to put to Parliament the documents and arguments with regard to the Dardanelles, which he was convinced would vindicate his actions. He was, however, able to avail himself, with regard to war policy, of a hitherto almost untested feature of parliamentary democracy in wartime—the Secret Session.

A Secret Session came into being by the device of the Speaker announcing, "I spy strangers." When he did so, all members of the public, distinguished strangers and journalists in the press galleries had to leave the Chamber. The Members of Parliament then debated and questioned Ministers, with no report of the session being made public, even in the official pages of *Hansard*.

At the Secret Session on 10 May 1917, called to debate criticisms of Lloyd George's war policy, the Asquith Liberals—the mere remnant of an Opposition party— were not ready to take the plunge. The main task of questioning the Government's policy fell to Churchill. In his speech, for which his own notes survive, he urged that no military offensives be carried out prematurely on the Western Front. The United States had entered the war on April 2, but American troops would not be ready for action until 1918. "Is it not obvious . . . ," Churchill asked, "that we should not squander the remaining armies of France and Britain in precipitate offensives before the American power begins to be felt on the battlefields?"

Churchill's plea was ignored. Within a few months the Third Battle of Ypres was launched, culminating in the bloodbath of Passchendaele.

As the First World War came to an end, Churchill, whom Lloyd George had made Minister of Munitions in 1917, wrote and spoke powerfully about the need to harness the same energies that war had generated to build a better peacetime Britain. He had earlier expressed this sentiment in 1900, as the war in South Africa was coming to an end. He was convinced that Parliament had the responsibility, as well as the means, to translate the energies of wartime into the impulses for peacetime reform.

A General Election was called for 14 December 1918. To his constituents at Dundee, Churchill set out the social policy he would like to see adopted by the postwar Parliament: the nationalization of the railways, the control of monopolies "in the general interest," and taxation levied "in proportion to the ability to pay." To Lloyd George, whose election at the head of a Liberal-Conservative coalition was certain, he wrote: "I do hope you will endeavour to gather together all forces of strength & influence in the country & lead them along the paths of science & organisation to the rescue of the weak & poor."

The Lloyd George coalition was victorious. Churchill was made Secretary of State for War and charged with the complex and urgent task of demobilization. Mutiny broke out three days after his appointment, due to the existing system. Churchill devised an equitable scheme based on the principle of "first in, first out."

The four years after the Armistice of 1918 saw some of Churchill's finest parliamentary expositions and achievements. As Secretary of State for War (1919–21), he upheld the Army Council's censure of General Dyer for the massacre of four hundred unarmed Indians at Amritsar, in the Punjab. Many Conservatives—the dominant group in Lloyd George's peacetime coalition—resented Churchill's attack on a British general. But Churchill, in one of his most impressive parliamentary performances, and to a largely hostile House, insisted that British rule in India must not be based on force. The shooting had been "a monstrous event." There was "one general prohibition" with regard to riots and civil strife that was essential: "a prohibition against what is called 'frightfulness.'"

"What I mean by frightfulness," Churchill explained, "is the inflicting of great slaughter upon a particular crowd of people, with the intention of terrorising not merely the rest of the crowd, but the whole district or the whole country. We cannot admit this doctrine in any form. Frightfulness is not a remedy known to the British pharmacopoeia." In Ireland, for which he had ministerial responsibility, his advice to the terrorists of Sinn Fein was succinct: "Quit murdering and start arguing."

From the War Office, Churchill went to the Colonial Office, where he worked for two years with intense energy to resolve the Irish conflict, dominated for the previous two years by civil war, terrorism, reprisal and counter-reprisal. In supporting a truce between Sinn Fein and the British government, Churchill prevailed on

Lloyd George to offer it without prior conditions. When the six counties of Ulster rejected any all-Irish settlement in which Sinn Fein would predominate, Churchill suggested the solution that was adopted and has lasted to this day: giving the South "the status of an Irish State," with a place in the League of Nations. His negotiations with the Sinn Fein leaders about the creation of the Irish Free State were masterpieces of tact and patience. A day after agreement was reached, he persuaded the Cabinet to waive the death penalty for those Sinn Feiners who had been convicted of murder and were still awaiting execution. "We had become allies and associates in a common cause," he later reflected. That cause was "peace between two races and two islands."

Churchill's speeches on the readings of the Irish Free State Bill—which enabled Southern Ireland to break free from British rule—were masterpieces of parliamentary presentation, as he led hostile Conservatives and sceptical Liberals carefully along the path of reason and logic towards the conclusion: Southern Ireland must be allowed to govern itself. One hitherto sceptical Conservative MP, Joseph Chamberlain's son Neville, told the House that it was Churchill's speech on the Ulster Boundary Commission that had made him "more convinced than ever" that the boundary would be drawn fairly.

On 31 March 1922 the Irish Free State Bill passed into law. The six counties of Ulster were to remain an integral part of Britain, henceforth designated "the United Kingdom of Great Britain and Northern Ireland." Throughout the negotiations and debates, and beyond them, Churchill acted as the conciliator between North and South, dependent on Parliament, and using all his parliamentary skills to establish a new national entity. "Tell Winston we could never have done anything without him," the head of the Free State Army, Michael Collins, told a friend. A few days later Collins was shot dead by dissidents of the Irish Republican Army. But the Treaty held, and the Free State survived.

5

The Democratic Process
Outside and Inside Parliament

T he success of parliamentary democracy depends not only on the workings of Parliament and the life within its walls but on the relationship between the members of each parliamentary assembly and those who elect them. The very process of being elected is an integral part of the democratic procedure on which parliamentary democracy depends.

On 19 October 1922, after the withdrawal of the support of the Conservative Party on which it depended, Lloyd George's coalition collapsed. Lloyd George resigned and the Conservative leader, Canadian-born Andrew Bonar Law, became Prime Minister. A General Election followed on November 15.

Churchill, having just had an operation for appendicitis, issued his election manifesto from his bed. He was standing, he said, "as a Liberal and a Free Trader." Although he managed, two days before polling day, to travel by night sleeper to his Dundee constituency and to speak to his constituents from a special chair—he was in too much pain to stand up—he was defeated. In a two-member constituency, he came fourth: the victors were the Prohibitionist and Labour Party candidates, and Churchill was without a seat in Parliament for the first time since 1901. Battered and bruised by defeat, Churchill quipped: "In an instant I was without a constituency, without a seat—and without an appendix." He was also without a place in Cabinet for the first time in eight years.

Churchill understood in 1922, as he would in 1945, that the electors expected more from their rulers than they had been getting, that their representatives in Parliament had failed them. T.E. Lawrence—Lawrence of Arabia, who had worked under him at the Colonial Office—wrote to him in sympathy and anger: "What bloody shits the Dundeans must be." But Churchill took a different view, writing to another friend: "If you saw the kind of lives the Dundee folk have to live, you would admit they have many excuses."

The 1922 General Election wiped out the Liberals as an effective governing instrument. The Conservatives, with 354 seats, were back in power for the first time since 1905. The second largest number of seats, 142, went to Labour, which for the first time became the predominant Opposition party. The Liberal Party had split, 62 seats going to Lloyd George's National Liberals and 54 seats to Asquith's followers. For the next decade and a half, with two short exceptions, parliamentary power would reside with the Conservatives.

For the previous seventeen years, Churchill had been a leading figure in the Liberal pantheon. Two weeks after his electoral defeat, he celebrated his forty-eighth birthday. He was still a Lloyd George Liberal. "The Whips will find me a seat if I wanted one," he wrote to a newly elected MP who had offered to stand down for him at Loughborough, "but what I want now is a rest."

In the months ahead, Churchill kept himself busy painting in the South of France, rebuilding the country home he had recently purchased at Chartwell, in Kent, and writing his First World War memoirs. In May 1924 he told a private dining club: "After seventeen years of rough official work, I can assure you that there are many things worse than public life."

Was Churchill still a Liberal? That May he lunched with Sir Robert Horne, a Conservative MP and former Chancellor of the Exchequer under Lloyd George. During the lunch, Horne asked Churchill where he stood politically. Churchill replied, according to Horne's report to a friend: "I am what I have always been—a Tory Democrat. Force of circumstance has compelled me to serve with another Party, but my views have never changed, and I should be glad to give effect to them by rejoining the Conservatives." Horne went so far as to suggest to the new Conservative leader, Stanley Baldwin, that Churchill be invited to join the Government, but although Baldwin was "impressed by the idea, he was doubtful about giving effect to it."

Baldwin did not forget Horne's suggestion. On 14 August 1923 he invited Churchill to 10 Downing Street. To avoid comment, Churchill entered the Prime Minister's residence by a side way, through the Treasury. After the meeting, he wrote to Clementine: "My talk with the PM was quite general & I did not raise the personal aspect at all at this preliminary & non-committal stage." His return to the Conservatives and to the Cabinet had, however, clearly been in both men's minds, although not discussed. Churchill's letter to his wife continued: "I shall proceed further before making up my mind."

There were rumours in political circles that the Conservatives intended to abandon Free Trade and to push for Protection—just as they had done, so disas-trously for themselves, almost two decades earlier. Churchill, still contemplating the possibility of office in a Conservative administration, was alarmed. In late September he saw the Conservative First Lord of the Admiralty, Leo Amery, and, Amery noted in his diary, "sounded me very anxiously about what our intentions were on the tariff issue, strongly urging us not to throw away a good position but to continue peacefully in office for the next two or three years." Churchill added, accord-ing to Amery's account, "that the Liberals were very anxious to have him back, but he was not having any, and was enjoying his present holiday immensely."

Six weeks after Churchill's talk with Amery, and before any further development could take place on

Churchill's potential return to the Conservatives, Stanley Baldwin announced that he was calling a General Election and that, if re-elected, the Conservatives would introduce Protection. Churchill, the Free Trade warrior of two decades earlier, the Free Trader of his 1922 election manifesto, was roused to action. Once more he wanted to be in Parliament to fight for the things he believed in. After publicly denouncing Protection as "a monstrous fallacy," he was approached by no fewer than seven constituencies, asking him to stand in the Liberal interest. The first of them was Glasgow Central.

On November 11 Churchill returned to the political arena, sending a letter to the newspapers stating that, while he would not stand at Glasgow, he would no longer be uncritical of the Conservatives—as he had been since the General Election a year earlier—because they had now levelled "an aggressive attack, needlessly and wantonly, at the foundations of the people's livelihood."

Five days later, in a speech at Manchester, Churchill appealed for the Lloyd George and Asquith Liberals to unite—under Asquith's leadership. In his speech he described Liberalism as the only "sure, sober, safe middle course of lucid intelligence and high principle."

Three days after his Manchester speech, Churchill agreed to stand as a Liberal at West Leicester. The Liberal Party had failed to unify, as he had hoped, and its electoral chances were poor. The election was held on December 6, a week after Churchill's forty-ninth birthday. He was defeated, gaining only 9,236 votes, compared with 13,634 for Labour. The Conservative candidate came third with 7,696.

Churchill much wanted to return to Parliament. His aunt Lady Sarah Wilson, one of his father's sisters, reported to him that even a "stodgy" old Tory had said to her, when the election result was announced: "Well, I am genuinely sorry. We wanted Winston in the House of Commons." The "stodgy" voice was that of Lord Midleton—the former St. John Brodrick against whom Churchill had conducted his first House of Commons battle twenty-two years earlier.

Following the 1923 General Election, Baldwin remained Prime Minister, but the Conservative seats had fallen from 346 to 258. Liberal and Labour combined had 349, a dangerous situation for the Conservatives should they combine.

That was exactly what they decided to do. Churchill, furious that the Liberals intended to work with Labour to bring down the Conservatives, and thereby to bring in a Labour Government, wrote to *The Times* that he refused to be party to "the enthronement in office of a Socialist Government." His letter constituted an effective public breach with the party in whose parliamentary ranks he had done so much over so many years for the good of so many people.

Churchill's letter was published on January 18. Three days later the Conservative Government was defeated in the House of Commons, and on the following morning the Leader of the Labour Party, Ramsay MacDonald, became Prime Minister. Churchill was appalled at the arrival of Britain's first Socialist Government. Yet the essence of parliamentary democracy was such that MacDonald and his party were now the governing power in Parliament, albeit dependent on Liberal Party support to survive.

Churchill hastened to congratulate MacDonald, who had entered the House of Commons in 1906; they had been fellow parliamentarians for sixteen years. His letter of congratulation has not yet been found, but from MacDonald's reply it is clear that Churchill had written to his political adversary in the true spirit of parliamentary democracy, setting political rancour aside and recognizing the importance of the task that had devolved upon his adversary. "No letter received by me at this time," MacDonald wrote in his own hand, "has given me more pleasure than yours. I wish we did not disagree so much! But there it is. In any event I hope your feelings are like mine. I have always held you personally in high esteem, & I hope, whatever fortune may have in store for us, that personal relationship will never be broken. Perhaps I may come across you occasionally."

Churchill was determined to return to the House of Commons, when, two weeks after the election, he was asked by the Liberal Association of Bristol West to stand as their candidate in the coming by-election, he declined, stating he would not be prepared "to embark upon a by-electoral contest against the Conservatives." Three weeks later, intervening in a by-election in Burnley, where a Conservative and a Labour candidate were contending, he urged Liberal voters not to vote for the Labour candidate. The *Glasgow Herald* commented: "Compelled by his temperament to be in the thick of the fighting, Mr Churchill seems a predestined champion of the individualism which he has served all his political life—under both of its liveries." His intervention at Burnley, the paper added, was without a doubt "preparing the way of return to the Party he left many years ago."

At the end of February 1924 a by-election was called for one of the most prestigious and overwhelmingly Conservative seats in London—the Abbey Division of Westminster. Churchill decided to announce his candidature as an "Independent Candidate" who would seek both Liberal and Conservative support. Although he had not been a member of the Conservative Party since 1904, he hoped that the local Conservative Association would adopt him as its candidate. Conservative Central Office was keen on this idea, seeing Churchill as the potential leader in the House of Commons of some thirty Liberal MPs who disliked the party's support for Labour, support that Asquith had encouraged.

Baldwin saw Churchill again at Downing Street. "He evidently wants very much to secure my return & co-operation," Churchill wrote to Clementine. But the local

Conservative Association did not fall in with either Central Office or the party Leader: instead, it adopted the nephew of the previous member as its candidate. Churchill faced the prospect of splitting the Conservative vote. But he was determined to try to get back to Parliament and felt confident he could win the seat. His private appeal to Baldwin to persuade the official Conservative candidate to stand down, or at least to ensure the "non-interference" of Conservative Central Office, was in vain. But his campaign effort in each of the nine wards in the constituency was headed by an existing Conservative MP.

One letter of support came from a former Conservative Prime Minister, Arthur Balfour, the object of so many of Churchill's criticisms in earlier years. "Your absence from the House of Commons at such a time," Balfour wrote, "is greatly to be deplored."

Churchill conducted a vigorous campaign. One proposal he advocated in the social sphere was the provision of houses "with proper State assistance." Novel methods and materials should be used, "in much the same way as the shell problem was solved during the war."

The result was incredibly close, so close that Churchill was initially believed to be the winner, to the delight of his supporters. But, in fact, the official candidate had won with 8,187 votes. Churchill was forty-three behind, a tiny margin. With 6,156 votes, the Labour candidate had failed to take advantage of the split. "You deserved to win," one Conservative MP wrote to Churchill when the result was known. "You are never more wanted in the House than now." Within two months of his defeat, Churchill went to Liverpool, where he made his first speech to a Conservative meeting in twenty years. There was no longer any place in British politics for an "independent" Liberal Party, he said. Only the Conservatives could defeat Labour. "Liberals" like himself, he said, must be prepared to support the Conservatives.

On 9 May 1924 the Ashton-under-Lyne Conservative Association asked Churchill to stand as an "Antisocialist" candidate. So too did the Conservatives at both Kettering and Royston. On May 10 Churchill informed Baldwin that he was helping to organize a group of Liberal MPs in the Commons to vote with the Conservatives on the next anti-Labour motion. At the end of the month he asked Baldwin to support his candidature at the second Westminster constituency, Westminster St. Georges. More than 1,500 of the electors there—though not the local Conservative Association—had urged him to stand, but Baldwin backed away. Finally, in July, the Conservative Central Office said that it would find Churchill a constituency and that he could stand, not as a Conservative—which he did not wish to do—but as a "Constitutionalist" candidate, with full Conservative support. Within a month he had been found a constituency, Epping, just outside London.

The General Election was held on 29 October 1924. Churchill faced both a Liberal and a Labour candidate. When the result was announced the following day he was once more a Member of Parliament, with 19,843 votes, compared with a combined total of 13,848 for his two opponents. Nationally, the Conservatives were returned to power with 419 seats, as against 151 for Labour. The Liberals had fallen to 40 seats. When Baldwin sent for Churchill, clearly to offer him a Cabinet post, Clementine suggested that he ask the Prime Minister for the Ministry of Health, where, Churchill later commented in a private note, "there was much to be done in housing and other social services with which in my Radical days I had been connected." To Churchill's astonishment, Baldwin asked him to become Chancellor of the Exchequer, the Cabinet position closest to the Prime Minister. Their residences in Downing Street were, and still are, adjacent, with a connecting inner door. Churchill accepted. For almost thirty years he had guarded his father's Chancellor's robes.

Baldwin had one request for his new Chancellor of the Exchequer: that he rejoin the Conservative Party. Churchill agreed. Henceforth he was to remain in the Conservative Party, to assume its leadership in 1940, and to represent it in Parliament for forty years.

As Chancellor of the Exchequer, Churchill was once again a central figure in the daily, practical workings of parliamentary democracy. A high point of the British parliamentary year is the Chancellor of the Exchequer's annual budget. Between 1925 and 1929, Churchill prepared and delivered five budgets, each of considerable stature. In his first, on 28 April 1925, he spoke for two hours and forty minutes. The measures he introduced included pensions for all widows and orphans, of whom 200,000 women and 350,000 children were the immediate beneficiaries. He also introduced a ten percent reduction in income tax for those in the lowest income groups.

Following the nine-day General Strike that began at midnight on 3 May 1926, Churchill took the lead in negotiations with the still-striking coal miners and the mine owners. Throughout the summer he made strenuous efforts to persuade the owners—including his cousin the Marquess of Londonderry—to give the miners a fair settlement. When the owners refused, Churchill wanted to introduce legislation to the House of Commons to force the owners to accept a national minimum wage for the miners. In secret talks at Chartwell with Ramsay MacDonald, and two days later in London with the miners' leaders, he asked them what would constitute a fair wage; then, in further talks with the owners, he produced that sum as if it were his own suggestion. It was Baldwin, hurrying back from his annual holiday in France, who supported the Cabinet's rejection of Churchill conciliation. Nor would the Cabinet support Churchill's suggestion, for which he had obtained the approval of the miners' leaders, for a compulsory arbitration tribunal.

Churchill introduced his third budget on 11 April 1927, resisting Cabinet pressure to ease the burden of death duties on the rich. A long-time Conservative opponent of Churchill, Lord Winterton, who had listened to the budget debate, wrote to a friend about Churchill's position in the House: "The remarkable thing about him is the way he has suddenly acquired, quite late in parliamentary life, an immense fund of tact, patience, good humour and banter on all occasions; no one used 'to suffer fools ungladly' more than Winston, but now he is friendly and accessible to everyone, both in the House and in the lobbies, with the result that he has become what he never was before the war, very popular in the House generally—a great accretion to his already formidable parliamentary power."

On 15 April 1929 Churchill introduced his fifth budget. It was a count reached previously only by Walpole, Pitt, Peel and Gladstone, each of whom was, or became, Prime Minister. Churchill spoke for almost three hours, setting out once more a substantial legislative plan. He abolished the duty on tea—a tax that had first been imposed in the reign of Queen Elizabeth I; removed railway passenger duty; ended the betting tax; reduced the duty on motorcycles and bicycles; imposed new duties on brewers, distillers and tobacco manufacturers; and announced an increase in Government spending on the telephone service, especially in rural areas.

In his diary, the Minister of Health, Neville Chamberlain, wrote that the speech had "kept the House fascinated and enthralled by its wit, audacity, adroitness and power."

Six weeks after Churchill's fifth budget, the Conservative Party was defeated at the General Election, and Britain's second Labour Government was voted into power. Churchill retained his seat at Epping and remained in Parliament, with a seat on the Conservative Shadow Cabinet: a Cabinet Minister in waiting. His faith in the parliamentary system was strong—he never saw it as being restricted to the island nation. Britain's most significant achievement, he had stated in 1927, was the "spread of the ideas of self-government, of personal liberty and of Parliamentary institutions throughout the world."

6

At Loggerheads with Parliament

Churchill's faith in parliamentary democracy was severely tested between 1929 and 1939, his decade out of political office—his "wilderness years," as they are known. He was often a lone voice then, especially on the issue of national defence. Yet throughout those years he was emphatic in asserting the supremacy of Parliament, first in making the decisions about imperial policy and the future of India, and then with regard to foreign affairs, the policy of rearmament, support for the Covenant of the League of Nations, and the need for alliances with other democratic states confronted by the growing threat of totalitarianism—as embodied from 1933 by Nazi Germany.

Speaking in Oxford in 1930, in the annual Romanes Lecture, Churchill urged his listeners to realize the importance of the parliamentary process for each generation: "I see the Houses of Parliament—and particularly the House of Commons—alone among the senates and chambers of the world a living and ruling entity; the swift vehicle of public opinion; the arena—perhaps fortunately padded arena—of the inevitable class and social conflict; the College from which the Ministers of State are chosen, and hitherto the solid and unfailing foundation of the executive power. I regard these parliamentary institutions as precious to us almost beyond compare. They seem to give by far the closest association yet achieved between the life of the people and the action of the state. They possess apparently an unlimited capacity of adaptiveness, and they stand an effective buffer against every form of revolutionary and reactionary violence." He then urged: "It should be the duty of all faithful subjects to preserve these institutions in their healthy vigour, to guard them against the encroachment of external forces, and to revivify them from one generation to another from the springs of national talent, interest, and esteem."

As the Nazi Party began making steady gains in the Reichstag, the German Parliament, there were those who pointed out, rightly, that the Reichstag was elected on a basis of universal suffrage, one man one vote, with a secret ballot, much on the British pattern. Indeed, it had been a condition of the establishment of the Weimar Republic in Germany in 1919 that it should be a parliamentary system. After the Second World War, in his war memoirs, Churchill noted that one of the "democratic provisions" of the Weimar Constitution prescribed biennial elections to the Reichstag—elections had to be held every two years. In Britain the statutory period was five years. By the two-year provision,

Churchill noted, it had been hoped "to make sure that the masses of the German people should enjoy a complete and continuous control over their Parliament. In practice, of course, it only meant that they lived in a continual atmosphere of febrile political excitement and ceaseless electioneering."

Such ceaseless electioneering proved to be a recipe for the emergence of extremism, linked as the electoral process was to continual street violence and intimidation. In the national election of 1928, Hitler secured a mere 12 seats in the Reichstag. Two years later the number rose to 107, and, two years after that, in 1932, to 230. A five-year system would have made such an outcome far less likely. The Weimar system of parliamentary democracy was a flawed one.

It was on the question of Britain's Imperial responsibilities that Churchill had his most difficult five years as a Member of Parliament. Throughout the India debates between 1929 and 1934, he looked to Parliament to take what he believed to be the right course. His major vexation from the outset of the discussions was that Stanley Baldwin, the Leader of the Conservative Party, without having a debate within the party, gave the Conservative Party's support to Ramsay MacDonald's India plans. Churchill, a member of the Conservative Shadow Cabinet and former Chancellor of Exchequer (often the stepping stone to the premiership), had not been consulted about this Conservative-Labour agreement, one that effectively removed India policy from meaningful parliamentary debate.

"So far as I could see," Churchill later reflected with some bitterness in his war memoirs, "Mr Baldwin felt that the times were too far gone for any robust assertion of British imperial greatness, and that the hope of the Conservative Party lay in accommodation with Liberal and Labour forces, and in adroit, well-timed manoeuvres to detach powerful moods of public opinion and large blocks of voters from them." Churchill added: "He was certainly very successful. He was the greatest Party manager the Conservatives ever had."

When Baldwin accepted MacDonald's plan for Indian self-government, Churchill resigned from the Shadow Cabinet on 27 January 1931. From that moment, for eight years and seven months, until the outbreak of war in September 1939, he was a backbench Member of Parliament, seeking to rally the relatively small number of Conservative MPs, seldom more than fifty, who were willing to go into the lobby with him to vote against the Government's India policy.

With the creation of the National Government in 1931, headed by Ramsay MacDonald but with a predominance of Conservative parliamentary support, Churchill sought to raise parliamentary concern at the India policy. When the National Government called for a vote of confidence in its India policy, it was Churchill who moved an amendment—not from the government benches, but from his seat of seniority on the front bench just below the ministerial section. No question of self-government in India, he asked, "shall impair the ultimate responsibility of parliament for the peace, order, and good government of the Indian Empire."

Fewer than fifty Members of Parliament supported Churchill's amendment. But at no point during the India debate did Churchill part company with his conviction that the will of the House of Commons was the sole arena for political change. Indeed, it was when he believed that the Government was acting dishonestly in putting forward its arguments for Indian constitutional reform that he called upon a rarely used parliamentary device—the Committee of Privileges.

Churchill did not believe that India, in 1934, was ready for parliamentary democracy. But he accepted absolutely that, with regard to India, the will of the British Parliament had to be respected. When the India Bill that he had opposed so strongly became law, he gave it his support, sending a message to Gandhi through the Mahatma's emissary and friend: "Tell Mr Gandhi to use the powers that are offered and make the thing a success. . . . You have got the thing now; make it a success, and if you do I will advocate your getting much more."

For Churchill the great strength of parliamentary democracy was the ability of parliamentarians to present an unpopular, or even a complex, case to a sceptical or puzzled audience and to make that case by clear argument and patient debate. He recognized, as did all parliamentarians, that one of the weaknesses of democracy lay in one of its particular strengths: that a good argument could be rejected; that the correct course—the moral course—could be turned down. Those elected by democratic means do not always have the highest good at the top of their agenda.

During the intensely fought appeasement debate, between 1933 and 1939, Churchill never despaired of parliamentary democracy, but his faith in it was severely tested. When Parliament supported the National Government's continuing disarmament proposals after Hitler had come to power in January 1933, even selling aircraft to Germany, Churchill was appalled at the unwillingness of the House of Commons to listen to his warnings of Germany's intention to become a dominant military power. "It is difficult to find a parallel," he wrote in his war memoirs, "to the unwisdom of the British and weakness of the French Governments, who none the less reflected the opinion of their Parliaments in this disastrous period."

Churchill saw it as his task to challenge the unwisdom of his British fellow parliamentarians. He spent hundreds of hours collecting and preparing the facts and statistics on which he based his speeches. In detailed warnings and appeals for a foreign policy that could find a way to prevent the onward march of German force, he advocated creating alliances with other threatened countries and working together within the Covenant of the League of Nations. That Covenant could mandate collective action against a potential aggressor.

This was a time of anguish for Churchill, confident that he was in the right but aware that it was only through Parliament that he could make his case and change the policies. "At Westminster," he later wrote in his war memoirs, "I pursued my two themes of India and the German menace, and went to Parliament from time to time to deliver warning speeches, which commanded attention, but did not, unhappily, wake to action the crowded, puzzled Houses which heard them."

It was not that Churchill lacked listeners in the Chamber. That aspect of parliamentary democracy served him well, even if the end results were disappointing. On one occasion, after the House had filled up to capacity to hear another of his powerful warnings about German intentions and the British lack of adequate response, a cynical MP called out: "Here endeth the Book of Lamentations." Quick as a flash another MP remarked: "Followed, it seems, by Exodus"—as the Chamber emptied out as soon as Churchill had finished speaking.

Both on India and on defence issues, Churchill was not alone among the senior figures in the Conservative

Party. "I found myself working in Parliament with a group of friends," he wrote in his war memoirs. These friends were influential party members who could, in his words, "at any time command the attention of Parliament and stage a full-dress debate."

On 16 February 1935 Churchill published an article in *Collier's* magazine entitled "Why Not Dictatorship." In it he wrote strongly against those in Europe, and even in Britain, who argued that dictatorship might be the best way forward for modern society. It was essential, in order to protect society "from the ambition, greed, malice or caprice of rulers," to ensure what he set out as the "inviolability of even the humblest home; the right and power of the private citizen to appeal to impartial courts against the State and against the Ministers of the day; freedom of speech and writing; freedom of the press; freedom of combination and agitation within the limits of long-established laws; the right of regular opposition to government; the power to turn out a government and put another set of men in its place by lawful, constitutional means; and finally the sense of association with the State and of some responsibility for its actions and conduct."

These were the elements underpinning parliamentary democracy that Churchill believed were essential for the well-being and, indeed, the survival of civilized society. It was also essential, he wrote, that the English-speaking peoples—above all those in Britain, Canada, Australia and New Zealand—first fight against "all this loose talk of dictatorships and one-man power. Secondly, they must guard with the utmost vigilance their own individual rights of citizenship. Thirdly, by the exercise of a far-seeing, enduring patience, they must submit themselves to the established and regular processes of law and make sure of fortifying the independence and impartiality of all who administer the law. Fourthly, they must acquaint themselves thoroughly with the past history of their country, reverence of its traditions, and take pride in the glorious achievement of their forefathers."

After giving a graphic account of the tyrannical nature of the Nazi regime in Germany, Churchill went on to ask:

Is there anything in all this which should lead us in the English-speaking world to repudiate the famous chain of events which has made us what we are?—to cast away our Parliament, our habeas corpus, our rights and many freedoms, our tolerances, our decencies? On the contrary, ought we not betimes to buttress and fortify our ancient constitutions, and to make sure that they are not ignorantly or lightly deranged?

What a lamentable result it would be if the British and American democracies, when enfranchised, squandered in a few short years or even between some night and morning all the long-stored, hard-won treasure of our common civilisation!

It must not be. If the present franchise were ever to be found incapable of defending the rights and liberties of British subjects or of American citizens against a vague and feckless mood of Caesarism, the franchise would have to be strengthened and weighted so as to assign due leadership to the more instructed and responsible elements.

Churchill had one caveat with regard to the existing franchise, which in Britain was then for both men and women over the age of twenty-one. "If we have gone too fast or too far in broadening the basis of full citizenship," he wrote, "and the result endangers the permanent well-being of the community, we must not hesitate to retrace our steps for a short distance. If our legislation as at present constituted does not give expression to the true strength of the nation, we must not fear or delay to make the necessary modification. The good cause must not perish through lack of proper organisation."

Churchill ended his *Collier's* article with a declaration of his faith in the existing British system. "Elected parliaments," he wrote, "in which all participate, with impartial courts of law and under a tradition-guarded constitution or limited monarchy, are the last words yet spoken in the honourable government of men."

Two months after this powerful appeal, which had been directed principally to readers in the United States, Churchill addressed a British readership, when, on 17 April 1935, he wrote an article in the *Daily Mail* headed, provocatively, "Is Parliament Merely a Talking

Shop?" "We must recognise that we have passed through a decade disastrous to Parliamentary institutions in almost every part of the world," he declared bluntly. "Democracy in so many lands is turning blindly but irresistibly to dictatorship. No virile, educated, scientific nation is going to let itself be let down or brought to a standstill by what is called 'Representative Government.'"

Churchill then wrote of the "amazing quality of the House of Commons is its power to digest, assimilate, conciliate, and tame all kinds of new elements," and he went on to express this idea in animal imagery with the words: "The Mother of Parliaments combines the fecundity of the rabbit with the digestion of the ostrich. But most of her progeny die of the diet, and already hardly any of the poor foreign sprigs survive."

It was in the context of the rise of dictatorships in Europe, and the dictatorial, aggressive government of Japan in the Far East, that Churchill wrote in his article for the *Daily Mail:* "There is no greater guarantee of our liberties than the House of Commons. Go at Question Time and listen to all the highest Ministers of State being questioned and cross-questioned on every conceivable subject and entering into the whole process with respect and with good will. Where else in the world can you see the representatives of democracy able to address the leading personages of a powerful government with this freedom?"

Seventy years later, Churchill might have written the same words. "How the foreigners gape at this performance when they visit the Gallery!" he wrote in his 1935 *Daily Mail* article. "What a sign it is that here the people own the Government, and not the Government the people." Churchill continued, of the House of Commons, that "in its scenes, in its sensations, in its turbulences, in its generosity, and above all in its native tolerance and decency . . . it is the august symbol and instrument of all that liberates and dignifies our island." Nevertheless, it would be folly to neglect the national defence. As he expressed it: "Ah! But guard these treasured privileges which are the envy of men of thought and culture in every quarter of the globe. Do not through folly or slothfulness let the citadel, not only of the British but of human rights and justice, be delivered defenceless to barbarian violence."

Churchill's article was a cry of pain—and also a cry of hope.

Writing again in the *Daily Mail* on 6 June 1935, less than two months later, when it seemed certain that an election would be held before the end of the year, Churchill pointed out that if the new Prime Minister were to form a Government "which offended the House of Commons, he and his colleagues could be dismissed in an afternoon, and someone else would have to try again to meet the wishes of the Assembly." If the House of Commons were to give its support to a Government "which the electorate did not like, this government could be swept away after the next general election." Therefore, public opinion, "expressed through all its hydra-heads, is master, and all the plans of the King's new Prime Minister must be attuned to the omnipresent, dominant influence. Here is our guarantee, here is our safeguard; it is all we have; but so far it has not failed."

———

The General Election was held on 14 November 1935. It was won, with a substantial majority, by the National Government, which insisted Nazi Germany posed no threat to Britain that could not be met my modest increases in defence spending and a continual search for agreement with the German dictator. Churchill disagreed emphatically with this view. As he saw it, and expressed it forcefully in debate, one essential strength of parliamentary democracy lay in the ability of elected representatives to challenge the mould of official self-deception and misinformation.

In his war memoirs, Churchill set down a strong condemnation of what he regarded as the failure of the 1935 Parliament to address the issue of defence with the vigour it demanded. He blamed all three political parties, Conservative, Labour and Liberal. Their collective conduct was, he wrote, "deeply blameworthy before history." History was not an abstraction for Churchill but a pointer to good or evil that could be anticipated. Yet the public did not always respond. "Unteachable from infancy to tomb, that is the first and main characteristic of mankind," he had written to a friend in 1927, after reading a history of the origins of the First World War.

———

As Hitler increased his military and air armament and imposed his racial anti-Jewish laws—laws that turned Jews into second-class citizens and outcasts within German society—several senior officials in the British Foreign Office discussed the failure of the Baldwin Government to explain to the public the profound conflict between the British and the Nazi ideologies. These officials, including the Permanent UnderSecretary of State for Foreign Affairs, Sir Robert Vansittart, feared that the desire for appeasement was leading to a lack of recognition of the deep divide between the democratic and the totalitarian systems. They approached Churchill and asked him if he would articulate these differences in a public speech that he was to give in Paris.

Churchill agreed, but when he sent the daft of his speech to the editor of *The Times*, the deputy editor, Robert Barrington-Ward, replied with a classic appeasement argument that *The Times* would "certainly be against any premature abandonment of the hope, supported by many authoritative pronouncements on the

German side, that Germany is prepared to reach a general understanding and settlement with the British Empire."

Churchill was convinced that, given the nature of the Nazi regime and the gulf between the democratic and totalitarian systems, no such understanding was possible. His Paris speech, delivered on 24 September 1936, was a clarion call in defence of parliamentary democracy. In the course of it he asked:

> How could we bear, nursed as we have been in a free atmosphere, to be gagged and muzzled; to have spies, eavesdroppers and delators at every corner; to have even private conversation caught up and used against us by the Secret Police and all their agents and creatures; to be arrested and interned without trial; or to be tried by political or Party courts for crimes hitherto unknown to civil law?
>
> How could we bear to be treated like schoolboys when we are grown-up men; to be turned out on parade to march and cheer for this slogan or that; to see philosophers, teachers and authors bullied and toiled to death in concentration camps; to be forced every hour to conceal the natural workings of the human intellect and the pulsations of the human heart?

There were still some people, Churchill commented, who saw no alternative to the two totalitarian systems of Nazism and Communism. This was not his view. As he told his Paris audience: "Between the doctrines of Comrade Trotsky and those of Dr. Goebbels there ought to be room for you and me, and a few others, to cultivate opinions of our own." Aggressive action should not be judged from the standpoint of Right and Left, but of "right and wrong." The democratic nations "are the guardians of causes so precious to the world that we must, as the Bible says, 'Lay aside every impediment' and prepare ourselves night and day to be worthy of the Faith that is in us."

Reflecting on Churchill's continued exclusion from government, one British newspaper commented: "We should like to hear Mr Churchill's defence of democracy reverberate from the sounding board of high office." But it was not to be. Both Stanley Baldwin and his successor, Neville Chamberlain, were convinced that some middle ground could be established whereby British democracy and German totalitarianism could find the means to live and work together. In Cabinet, on 7 November 1936, the Minister for the Co-ordination of Defence, Sir Thomas Inskip, suggested that, in place of the support for the collective security of threatened States—as envisaged by the League of Nations and strongly urged by Churchill—a policy aimed at "the appeasement of Germany's economic conditions" would be one "for which there was some hope."

While not informed of this specific suggestion, Churchill knew that the arguments in favour of collective security—of rearmament and recourse to the Covenant of the League of Nations—were not supported by the Cabinet. "All I can say," he told the House of Commons on the day after Inskip's remark, "is that unless there is a front against potential aggression there will be no settlement. All the nations of Europe will just be driven helter-skelter across the diplomatic chessboard of Europe until the limits of retreat are exhausted, and then out of desperation, perhaps in some most unlikely quarter, the explosion of war will take place, probably under conditions not very favourable to those who have been engaged in this long retreat."

On 11 November 1936 Churchill moved an amendment stating that Britain's defences were no longer adequate to face the threat of war. One suggestion he put forward was a Ministry of Supply, so that the government could coordinate the preparation and expansion of war industries. The Government had said that it was "always reviewing the position." "Anyone can see what the position is," Churchill declared. "The Government simply cannot make up their mind . . . So they go on in strange paradox, decided only to be undecided, resolute to be irresolute, adamant for drift, solid for fluidity, all powerful to be impotent." But his real accusation was against his fellow MPs:

I have been staggered by the failure of the House of Commons to react effectively against these dangers. That, I am bound to say, I never expected.

I never would have believed that we should have been allowed to go on getting into this plight, month by month and year by year, and that even the Government's own confessions of error would have produced no concentration of Parliamentary opinion and force capable of lifting our efforts to the level of emergency.

I say that unless the House resolves to find out the truth for itself it will have committed an act of abdication of duty without parallel in its long history.

Here was one of the weaknesses in parliamentary democracy: the rigidity of the party system. Throughout the 1930s, Churchill spoke strongly in Parliament against Members voting according to their party leaders, even when they were known to be personally uneasy about the party line.

Churchill saw a second weakness in parliamentary democracy during the appeasement decade: the power of political leaders to deceive the public—to win votes, to win elections, and to come to power on false policies, and to maintain power on false information, and disinformation, to the detriment of national security.

Many of Churchill's presentations in the House of Commons exposed the gap between the situation as described by the government and the actual situation, as he was able to present it to the House. With regard to German rearmament and British defence capacity, his speeches were often based on the very statistics that the government had been given in secrecy from its own experts, but had chosen to fudge or ignore. "I have been mocked and censured as a scaremonger and even as a warmonger," Churchill told his constituents on 20 June 1936, "by those whose complacency and inertia have brought us all nearer to war and war nearer to us all. But I have the comfort of knowing that I have spoken the truth and done my duty. . . . Indeed I am more proud of the long series of speeches which I have made on defence and foreign policy in the last four years than of anything I have ever been able to do, in all my forty years of public life."

Churchill never gave up making his points in the Chamber. "The House of Commons," he declared on 31 May 1937, "still survives as the arena of free debate." But the fact that the House was being deceived and mis-informed on a wide range of defence and security issues caused Churchill deep distress. Recalling the 25 April 1938 debate on the British naval bases in western Ireland—bases that Churchill himself had secured for Britain in the Irish Treaty of 1922, and which Neville Chamberlain transferred to the Republic of Ireland, thus denying them to Britain in any future war—Churchill later noted, in his war memoirs: "I was listened to with a patient air of scepticism. I never saw the House of Commons so completely misled."

Realizing, and accepting the centrality of Parliament in the appeasement debate, Churchill spoke in the House at each stage and on each issue, hoping to convince more and more of his fellow Members that the appeasement policy could only lead to war from a position of weakness. Slowly, his arguments were taken seriously and began to influence an increasing number of Members. Malcolm MacDonald, Ramsay MacDonald's son and a member of Chamberlain's Cabinet, later told me how, during Churchill's sustained indictment on 5 October 1938 of the Munich Agreement, his palms were wet with sweat as he realized the force of Churchill's warnings.

Despite the many Members of Parliament who spoke against the Munich Agreement during the three-day debate, the policy did not change. Nor, when he again advocated setting up a Ministry of Supply during a debate on 17 November 1938, could Churchill overcome the pressures of the Party Whips. From his seat on the front bench, he turned round to face the serried ranks of Conservative MPs and told them: "Hon. Gentlemen above the gangway—pledged loyal, faithful supporters on all occasion of His Majesty's Government—must not imagine that they can throw the burden wholly on the Ministers of the Crown. Much power has rested with them. One healthy growl from those benches three years ago—and how different today would be with the whole layout of our armament production. Alas, that service was not forthcoming."

It was not a party question, Churchill declared. It had "nothing to do with Party." It was "entirely an issue affecting the broad safety of the nation." Churchill's call for an independent stance was a total failure. He hoped that fifty Conservative MPs would defy the Whip and join him in the lobby. Not fifty, but two, went with him. One of them was his friend Brendan Bracken; the other was a future Conservative Prime Minister, Harold Macmillan.

Churchill did not know where to turn. If Parliament could not alter the policy, he knew no alternative method. Even his own attempts to rally public opinion, through speeches and newspaper articles, were, he felt, of no avail. It was Parliament that had to speak. But Conservative Central Office was trying to remove him from that essential forum, almost four decades after he had first taken his seat. An attempt was being made by the party organizers to have him de-selected from his Epping constituency. When, as a Christmas gift, the Leader of the Ulster Unionists, Viscount Craigavon—who, as James Craig, had negotiated the 1922 Irish Treaty with Churchill—sent him an engraved silver cup as a token of appreciation, Churchill wrote to Clementine: "I wish some of these dirty Tory hacks, who would like to drive me out of the Party, could see this trophy."

There were those who urged Churchill to form a new political party, to challenge the government. "I am sure," he wrote to one such suggestion, "if there were any reasonable alternative to the present Government, they would be chased out of power by the country. But the difficulties of organising and forming a new party have often proved insuperable."

In December 1938, as the dictator powers of Europe were each week gaining in confidence and arrogance, Churchill set out in the *News of the World*—on December 18—the case for the parliamentary system. Not only in the House of Commons but on the hustings it was the essential bulwark of democracy. "I have seen many excited election crowds in England where everyone is apparently in a frenzy," he wrote. "You see their faces convulsed with anger, but there seems to be a great inhibition against actually striking a public man. This is as it should be. There ought to be intense feeling kept under proper restraint." For this reason, Churchill explained, after "all my years of rough fighting at elections," he could repeat "with the greatest confidence" his father's declaration: "I never feared the English democracy."

In this article, Churchill contrasted the power and independence of the House of Commons of earlier years with the House in 1938. In earlier years, he argued, it was "a far more living powerful entity in our national life than it is now." Churchill believed that the overwhelming numerical strength of a single party, such as the Conservatives under Neville Chamberlain, could lead to weakness in the democratic process. That process, as seen in the contrast between the serried ranks of the Government benches and the much-reduced Opposition benches, could strengthen rigidity of doctrine, especially when two points of view were at loggerheads: appeasers with their overwhelming parliamentary majority, and anti-appeasers, despite the strength of their convictions, always a minority on both the Government and the Opposition benches.

In such a circumstance, parliamentary democracy had its sinister opponents, including those in Churchill's own party at Conservative Central Office, who, at the end of 1938, continued to seek to de-select him from his constituency, so that he would no longer be a Member of Parliament. He was distressed that an attempt should be made to remove him at such a low ebb in the influence of the few independent-minded members. "It is remarkable," he wrote in the *News of the World* on 1 January 1939, "that at a time when parliamentary institutions are most threatened, they are themselves at the lowest ebb. We do not have any longer the clash of debate, and the confrontation by effective champions of great bodies of organised opinion. In the main it is the Government of the day contending, none too well, with overwhelming preponderant difficulties, and the rest of the House either backing them up or making a formal effort at criticism."

Churchill stressed in this article the need to maintain good relations in the House of Commons between men and women of all parties and points of view. Reflecting on the crisis between the democratic and anti-democratic nations, he wrote: "Our institutions threatened, on trial, and to some extent in eclipse in this harsh totalitarian world, depend for their life and vigour mainly upon good feeling and decent behaviour." It was the public who were

most endangered by an intensification of political conflict beyond the civilities of the House of Commons. "The
only foundation for good government and happy results
for the people," he wrote, "is a high standard of com-
radeship and fellowship between those who are called
upon to handle their affairs."

The 1930s was a period in which there were people
even in Britain who argued that totalitarianism was
preferable to democracy. Both Communism and Fascism
had their advocates in many parliamentary countries:
indeed, several European countries had succumbed to, or
were dallying with, dictatorial systems. The question
remained, in Churchill's mind, "whether our ancient
Parliamentary institutions can survive." They would be
able to do so, he wrote, only "if they show themselves
capable of upholding the same national discipline and
intense effort for survival which are undoubtedly realised
in the Dictator States." In times of danger, "sacrifice
and common exertion" would be required. "But we must
still hope that the House of Commons, although it no
longer represents the strong life force of the nation, but
rather a vague, floating, half-focused public opinion, will
nevertheless rise to the level of its dangers, and prove
itself a worthy inheritor of the great traditions and
achievement which have called it into being."

These high hopes were not to be realized until the
coming of war nine months later. Meanwhile, to
Churchill's distress, Conservative Central Office made

a second attempt to find a would-be Conservative candidate to challenge him in his constituency, so that, if defeated in the party caucus, he would have to leave the House of Commons altogether. On 10 March 1939 he asked his fellow Members of Parliament: "What is the value of our Parliamentary institutions, and how can our Parliamentary doctrines survive, if constituencies tried to return only tame, docile and subservient members who tried to stamp out every form of independent judgement?"

One of Churchill's favourite Gilbert and Sullivan couplets comes to mind, from *HMS Pinafore,* in which "the ruler of the Queen's Navee"—a post that Churchill held twice as First Lord of the Admiralty—explains how he rose to such a prominent position in government:

I always voted at my Party's call.

I never thought of thinking for myself at all.

On 22 May 1939, two months after lamenting "the tame, docile and subservient members" during a debate on the government's restriction of Jewish immigration to Palestine, Churchill commented on the fact that the "supreme argument" on which the government was relying was the Three-Line Whip—the order for all party members to attend and to vote. This, he pointed out, had been brought in only after a poor performance by the Minister defending the Government's policy: "Not only the Landwehr but the Landsturm were called out. That was not because the case was found to be exceptionally strong. It was because the case was weak, and because it was thought necessary to override arguments by a parade of numbers."

Churchill found all such tampering with parliamentary democracy detrimental to what he believed were the strengths it had acquired after many centuries of conflict, civil war, and the slow but steady evolution of parliamentary procedure. This view, gained by a wide reading in British history, including his father's part in it, was reinforced by his practical experiences of the workings of Parliament in peace and war. He refined it between 1936 and 1939 as he wrote his four-volume book, *A History of the English-speaking Peoples.*

On 12 April 1939, as war clouds loomed, he wrote to one of his literary assistants about that history he was writing: "In the main, the theme is emerging of the growth of freedom and law, of the rights of the individual, of the subordination of the State to the fundamental and moral conceptions of an ever-comprehending community. Of these ideas the English-speaking peoples were the authors, then the trustees, and must now become the armed champions. Thus I condemn tyranny in whatever guise and from whatever quarter it presents itself. All this of course has a current application."

On 18 April 1939 Neville Chamberlain finally agreed to establish a Ministry of Supply, to coordinate industrial production in the event of war. "Winston has won his long fight," Brendan Bracken wrote to a friend. "Our Government are now adopting the policy he advised three years ago. No public man in our time has shown more foresight, and I believe that his long, lonely struggle to expose the dangers of dictatorships will prove to be the best chapter in his crowded life."

As Churchill saw it, parliamentary democracy and dictatorship not only stood at opposite poles but had no common ground. Democracy had to defend itself. "Appeasement from weakness and fear is alike futile and fatal," he told the House of Commons on 14 December 1950, during a debate on the Korean War. "Appeasement from strength is magnanimous and noble, and might be the surest and perhaps the only path to world peace." It was to oppose the "futile and fatal" form of appeasement that he had fought so hard in Parliament after Hitler had come to power.

The idea of the abdication by Parliament of its responsibilities was abhorrent to Churchill: hence his objections to the two-month adjournment of the House of Commons that the Government instituted on 2 August 1939. There was, Churchill warned the House, "a definite movement" of German troops and supplies through Austria "towards the east." Angrily he continued: "At this moment in its long history it would be disastrous, it would be pathetic, it would be shameful for the House of Commons to write itself off as an effective and potent factor in the situation, or to reduce whatever strength it can offer to the firm front which the nations will make against aggression. . . ."

Chamberlain would not agree to let the House remain in session. Within a month of the adjournment, Hitler invaded Poland, and both Britain and France declared war on Germany. The rights of the individual were trampled upon by Hitler from the first days of the invasion of Poland. "This is no war," Churchill told the House of Commons in his first wartime speech, "of domination or imperial aggrandizement or material gain; no war to shut any country out of its sunlight and means of progress. It is a war, viewed in its inherent quality, to establish, on impregnable rocks, the rights of the individual, and it is a war to establish and revive the stature of man."

7

Parliament in Time of Total War

The greatest challenge to parliamentary democracy is the threat of defeat at the hands of a dictator regime. It is to avert the curse of totalitarian rule that parliamentary democracy asserts itself as the essential governing system. Yet, faced by the threat of military aggression and defeat, Parliament itself has to accept a diminution of its authority, as harsh measures are required to secure national survival.

On 10 May 1940, as German forces invaded Belgium, Holland and France, Churchill became Prime Minister. He at once brought the leading figures of the opposition Labour and Liberal parties into central positions of war policy and war direction. By this act, he ensured that the elected representatives of the people across the political spectrum would have whatever say in the conduct of the war that would be vouchsafed to Parliament.

As Belgium, Holland and France succumbed to the German assault, a German invasion of Britain seemed imminent. Churchill realized that Britain's democracy—Britain's way of life—was in danger of destruction and that, to preserve democracy, some democratic rights had to be suspended. That was done, but done through Parliament. Imprisonment without trial was instituted by a series of parliamentary votes in a single day. Newspaper censorship was put in place. Tens of thousands of German Jewish refugees from Hitler were interned, for fear that there might be fifth columnists, however few, among them: the rapid German conquest of Holland that very week had been ascribed in part to German Fifth Column activity. Parliament agreed that war—and the possibility of defeat in war—called for stern measures.

Britain and, with it, British parliamentary democracy were under the threat of physical attack. Within a few months, six parliamentary governments had been overthrown by Nazi Germany. Churchill saw the war not only as a means of preserving Britain's independence, and in due course defeating the enemy, but as a struggle for the preservation of parliamentary institutions and democratic values worldwide. On 12 August 1941 he and President Franklin D. Roosevelt, meeting off Newfoundland, issued the Atlantic Charter, a series of pledges offering all nations of the world democracy and freely elected Parliaments.

One sentence in the Atlantic Charter reflected Churchill's hopes for democracy in all lands under tyranny. It pledged Britain and the United States to "respect the rights of all peoples to choose the form of government under which they will live; and they wish to see sovereign rights and self-government restored to those who have been forcibly deprived of them." To this end, Churchill was to spend many hours arguing with the Soviet leader, Josef Stalin, to try to restore democracy to Poland after the war. But while Churchill had the ideals, Stalin had the tanks.

Stalin was full of scorn for democracy and religion. On one occasion, when Churchill asked him to grant religious rights to Roman Catholics, he replied, derisively, "How many Divisions has the Pope?" Of course the Pope had no soldiers as such, beyond the Vatican's Swiss Guard. But, like Churchill, the Vatican had a belief in the force of morality and decency.

As Prime Minister, Churchill made regular, detailed reports to Parliament on the course of the war. He made great efforts, by his presence in the Chamber, to raise the morale of Parliament during the prolonged blitz and bombardment. His Junior Private Secretary, John "Jock" Colville, noted in his diary on 22 January 1941 how Churchill did "extremely well" in explaining a complex new administrative arrangement, speaking "with the utmost clearness and cogency." Churchill took great trouble at every stage to keep Parliament informed and at ease, amid grave events and frequent setbacks on land and at sea. To his son, Randolph, then serving at army headquarters in Egypt, Churchill wrote in June 1941 of how, two days before the Chamber was destroyed by bombing in May, "I had a most successful debate and wound up amid a great demonstration. They all got up and cheered as I left."

Churchill did not hesitate to explain the primacy of the House of Commons when he was overseas. During his first speech to a Joint Session of the United States Congress, on 26 December 1941—on his first wartime visit to the United States—he told the American legislators: "I am a child of the House of Commons. I was brought up in my father's house to believe in democracy. Trust the people—that was his message. . . . I cannot help reflecting that if my father had been American and my mother British, instead of the other way around, I might have got here on my own. . . . I owe my advancement entirely to the House of Commons, whose servant I am. In my country, as in yours, public men are proud to be the servants of the State and would be ashamed to be its masters."

Four days after this speech to Congress, Churchill was in Ottawa, where he addressed the Canadian Parliament. One point he made, in his inimitable way, was that parliamentary democracies did not have to be weak and vulnerable. As he told the Canadian legislators: "We have not journeyed all this way across the centuries, across the oceans, across the mountains, across the prairies, because we are made of sugar candy." Neither the length of the struggle, "nor any form of severity it may assume, shall make us weary or shall make us quit."

Canada had no intention of quitting. Churchill knew of Canada's contribution to the war effort. More than a hundred Canadian pilots had flown in the Battle of Britain. In the many battles that lay ahead, nearly one thousand Canadian soldiers were to be killed at Dieppe, and a further five thousand in Sicily and Italy. In the Normandy landings, 358 gave their lives. Thousands more were to be killed in the fight for the liberation of France, Belgium, and Holland in 1945. Canadian sailors and merchant seamen faced, from the first days of the war, all the perils of the war at sea.

Churchill returned to Canada in 1943 to confer at Quebec with Roosevelt and the Canadian Prime Minister William Lyon Mackenzie King. In a later broadcast from Quebec on 31 August 1943 Churchill declared: "Here at the gateway to Canada, in mighty lands which have never known the totalitarian tyrannies of Hitler and Mussolini, the spirit of freedom has found a safe and abiding home." Because the Soviet Union was an Allied Power, he could not with prudence include Stalin in his list of dictators.

War created situations in which the workings of Parliament were hampered and frustrated, not least because so many Members, including Churchill's son, Randolph, were serving in the armed forces far from home. Contested by-elections were suspended, since electioneering was not practicable in wartime. The bombing of the Chamber forced the debates to be held elsewhere—

at Church House, Westminster. The secrecy of so many matters meant a resort to the Secret Sessions, as had happened during the First World War, with no report of the debate being made public. "Thus we arrive," Churchill told the House on 8 September 1942, "by our ancient constitutional methods, at practical working arrangements which show that Parliamentary democracy can adapt itself to all situations and can go out in all weathers."

Jock Colville, who served in Churchill's Private Office in both his premierships, commented that, even at the height of his power, "when he could have got away with almost anything," Churchill always reported to the House of Commons "the main principles accepted by the Cabinet on matters affecting the conduct of the war, and told the House of the results, good or bad, that had been achieved. Having done so, he asked the House of Commons for its approval and never shrank from a vote of censure." "I am," he used to say, "the servant of the House of Commons."

As setbacks and defeats marked the desperate course of the war, Churchill spoke with confidence about the role of the House of Commons, telling Members of Parliament about their bombed and battered institution on 23 October 1942: "There is no situation to which it cannot address itself with vigour and ingenuity. It is the citadel of British liberty. It is the foundation of our laws."

Churchill explained to Roosevelt: "Democracy has to prove that it can provide a granite foundation for war against tyranny." The preservation and enhancement of democracy was an integral part of Churchill's war leadership, a vision of the world that would follow an Allied victory. Upholding democratic values, both in Britain and throughout postwar Europe, where democracies had been submerged by Fascism and Nazism, became a task and a call. "It was Parliament," Churchill told his fellow parliamentarians—many of whom were serving officers—that constituted "the shield and expression of democracy," and it was in Parliament that "all grievances or muddles or scandals, if such there be," should be debated.

Even in 1940, when defeat seemed sure, the democratic way of life was maintained. Indeed, from 1940 to 1945 Churchill made certain that this was so. At the height of the war, Parliament met regularly. It debated vigorously and critically. On 1 July 1942, as German forces penetrated 130 miles inside Egypt and only 40 miles from Cairo, a full-scale Vote of Censure debate took place in the House of Commons. The debate was called by a Conservative MP, Sir John Wardlaw-Milne, who argued, as did his supporters in the House, that a more effective war leader was needed. On the second day of the debate the Labour left-winger Aneurin Bevan told the House: "The Prime Minister wins debate after debate and loses battle after battle. The country is beginning to say that he fights debates like a war and the war like a debate."

The moment in the debate had come when Churchill would have to speak. "I said a little prayer for him as he went off," his secretary Elizabeth Layton wrote to her parents in Canada. Churchill spoke of the nature and conduct of the war and of his own efforts "under the supervision and control of the War Cabinet"—a true statement of the restrictions on his power of action. He went on to explain that nearly all his work had been done in writing and that "a complete record exists of all the directions I have given, all the enquiries I have made, and the telegrams I have drafted." And, he added, "I shall be perfectly content to be judged by them."

Churchill said that he asked "no favours." He had undertaken the office of Prime Minister and Minister of Defence in May 1940, after defending Neville Chamberlain's conduct of the war thus far "to the best of my ability" and at a time when the life of the British Empire "hung upon a thread." He went on to declare: "I am your servant and you have the right to dismiss me when you please. What you have no right to do is to ask me to bear responsibilities without the power of effective action."

Churchill did not mince his words. "If democracy and Parliamentary institutions are to triumph in this war," he said, "it is absolutely necessary that Governments resting upon them shall be able to act and dare, that the servants of the Crown shall not be harassed by nagging and snarling, that enemy propaganda shall not be fed needlessly out of our own hands and our reputation disparaged and undermined throughout the world."

A motion of No Confidence was called—it was defeated by 475 votes to 25. Parliament had spent two days in unfettered and public criticism. The newspapers—despite the necessary wartime censorship—were equally free to criticize, and they did so frequently. On 28 October 1943 Churchill told the House of Commons, the Chamber of which had been destroyed during a German bombing raid on London on the night of 10 May 1941: "Our House has proved itself capable of adapting itself to every change which the swift pace of modern life has brought upon us. It has a collective personality which enjoys the regard of the public, and which imposes itself upon the conduct not only of individual Members but of Parties. It has a code of its own which everyone knows, and it has means of its own of enforcing those manners and habits which have grown up and have been found to be an essential part of our Parliamentary life."

Churchill was also concerned that, when the Chamber was eventually rebuilt, it should be on the former pattern. As he told the House, which was then sitting in the undamaged Chamber of the House of Lords: "We shape our buildings and afterwards our buildings shape us.

Having dwelt and served for more than forty years in the late Chamber, and having derived very great pleasure and advantage therefrom, I, naturally, would like to see it restored in all essentials to its old form, convenience and dignity. I believe that will be the opinion of the majority of its Members."

With regard to the destroyed Chamber and parliamentary democracy, Churchill had another point to make: "We are building warships," he said, "that will not be finished for many years ahead, and various works of construction are going forward for war purposes. But I am bound to say that I rank the House of Commons—the most powerful Assembly in the whole world—at least as important as a fortification or a battleship, even in time of war. Politics may be very fierce and violent in the after-war days. We may have all the changes in personnel following upon a General Election. We shall certainly have an immense press of business and, very likely, of stormy controversy. We must have a good, well-tried and convenient place in which to do our work. The House owes it to itself, it owes it to the nation, to make sure that there is no gap, no awkward, injurious hiatus in the continuity of our Parliamentary life."

In wartime, the powers of Parliaments, as of all democratic legislative assemblies, are necessarily curbed by the urgent, often highly secret, daily demands of war-making. But Churchill did not want this fact to eclipse or weaken the importance of parliamentary systems or the regard in which those systems were held. During one of his wartime visits to the United States, he expressed his view of democracy in these words: "These ideas of Parliamentary government, of the representation of the people upon franchises, which extend as time goes on, and which in our country have reached the complete limits of universal suffrage, these institutions and principles constitute at this moment one of the great causes which are being fought out in the world. With all their weakness and with all their strength, with all their faults, with all their virtues, with all the criticism that may be made against them, with their many shortcomings, with lack of foresight, lack of continuity of purpose, or pressure only of superficial purpose, they nevertheless assert the right of the common people—the broad masses of the people—to take a conscious effective share in the government of their country."

This speech was not mere rhetoric: Churchill's words always meant what they said in practical terms. When, in March 1944, there was a mini-revolt on a progressive piece of domestic legislation, the Education Bill, he insisted on a full-scale debate. "I have had some little trouble here, which has been coming to a head for some time," he telegraphed to Roosevelt, "which forced me to fall back upon the House of Commons, which as usual

showed itself steadfast in the cause and put all the malig-
nants in their proper places." To his son, Randolph, he
wrote more colloquially: "I am the child of the H of C, and
when I was molested by a number of cheeky boys, I ran
for succour to the old Mother of Parliaments, and she
certainly chased them out of the backyard with her mop."

On 4 April 1944 Churchill told the House of Commons:
"It must be remembered that the function of Parliament
is not only to pass good laws, but to stop bad laws." He
was content that the parliamentarians were vigilant
with regard to all legislation, as he had been when in
Opposition.

———

In the summer of 1944, shortly after Allied troops liberated Rome, Churchill was asked to set out for the
Italian people the ideas that should guide them now
that Italian Fascism had been overthrown—the harsh,
totalitarian rule of Mussolini and his Fascist Party.
Churchill's message reflects his abiding personal concern for the restoration and preservation of democratic
principles, wherever peoples and governments were prepared to uphold them. Echoing his *Collier's* article of
nine years earlier, he wrote, on 28 August 1944:

Is there the right to free expression of opinion and of
opposition and criticism of the Government of the day?

Have the people the right to turn out a government of which they disapprove, and are constitutional means provided by which they can make their will apparent?

Are their courts of justice free from violence by the Executive and from threats of mob violence, and free of all association with particular political parties?

Will these courts administer open and well-established laws which are associated in the human mind with the broad principles of decency and justice?

Will there be fair play for poor as well as for rich, for private persons as well as government officials?

Will the rights of the individual, subject to his duties to the State, be maintained and asserted and exalted?

Is the ordinary peasant or workman who is earning a living by daily toil and trying to bring up a family free from the fear that some grim police organization under the control of a single party, like the Gestapo, started by the Nazi and Fascist parties, will tap him on the shoulder and pack him off without fair or open trial to bondage or ill treatment?

"These simple, practical tests," Churchill added, "are some of the title-deeds on which a new Italy could be founded." Ten years later, when he printed these questions in his war memoirs, Churchill noted: "This does not seem to require any alteration today."

As much as the Atlantic Charter of three years earlier, these questions to the Italian people were a mark and a proof of the ultimate objective of Churchill's war leadership: faith in democracy, the need to preserve democracy, and the hope of returning democracy to those countries that had been deprived of it by the victories of totalitarianism. Two months after his questions to the Italian people, Churchill told the House of Commons, on 31 October 1944: "The foundation of all democracy is that the people have the right to vote. To deprive them of that right is to make a mockery of all the high-sounding phrases which are so often used. At the bottom of all the tributes paid to democracy is the little man, walking into the little booth, with a little pencil, making a little cross on a little bit of paper—no amount of rhetoric or voluminous discussion can possibly diminish the overwhelming importance of that point."

In December 1944, when democracy was under grave threat in liberated Greece in the form of a civil war, Churchill flew personally to Athens, to persuade the warring Greek factions to accept a unified, parliamentary-based government. In justifying his personal intervention, he told the House of Commons: "Democracy is no harlot to be picked up in the street by a man with a Tommy gun. I trust the people, the mass of the people, in almost any country, but I like to make sure that it is the people and not a gang of bandits from the mountains or from the countryside who think that by violence they can overturn constituted authority, in some cases ancient Parliaments, Governments and States."

In a telegram to Roosevelt, Churchill turned to another Balkan country in danger of a Communist takeover. "We should insist as far as is possible," he wrote, "on full and fair elections deciding the future regime of the Yugoslav people or peoples."

It was not only the Italian and Greek peoples for whom Churchill sought a democratic and parliamentary future. From the first days of the war, which had begun with the German invasion of Poland, he regarded the restoration of a democratic Poland, based on the "free vote of the Polish people," as an essential Allied war aim. He spent as many hours—in Moscow in 1942 and 1944, and at Yalta and Potsdam in 1945—pressing upon Stalin the need for a post-war independent Poland, as he spent on any other single issue.

Churchill regarded Stalin's betrayal of the Big Three pledge at Yalta for "free elections" in Poland as a moment of truth and the start of the Cold War. But he had faith that democracy would return to Poland. "Peoples in bondage should never despair," he declared four years after the Soviet Union imposed a Communist regime on Poland. He went on to explain: "The machinery of propaganda may pack their minds with falsehood and deny them truth for many generations of time, but the soul of man thus held in trance, or frozen in a long night, can be awakened by a spark coming from God knows where, and in a moment the whole structure of lies and oppression is on trial for its life."

Forty-two years after Churchill spoke these words, and twenty-six years after his death, the Iron Curtain fell, and democratic parliaments were restored not only in Poland, but throughout the former satellite states.

8

Setbacks, Recovery and
an Enduring Faith

For the workings of parliamentary democracy, the transition from wartime to peacetime, after five-and-a-half years, was not an easy one. Yet the instincts of parliamentary procedure and the paramountcy of the electoral process were able to survive and flourish as soon as the dark cloud of war was lifted. The process whereby this happened, and the result of the change from war to peace in 1945, are an object lesson in the resilience of parliamentary democracy and its essential superiority over the internal convulsions created by the dictatorial and totalitarian systems.

As the war in Europe drew to its end, Churchill envisaged maintaining his all-party coalition for a least a year after the defeat of Germany, hoping to use the combined, united force of the nation's political parties to establish decent peacetime conditions for all. Among the measures he had in mind was a National Health Service, outlined in 1943 in the Government's Four-Year Plan. He had been disappointed in 1918 when Lloyd George had not responded to his similar vision for the use of wartime organizations and energies to push forward domestic social reforms.

The war with Germany ended on 8 May 1945. Ten days later Clement Attlee went to see Churchill to tell him that he was "favourably disposed" to maintaining the coalition. So too were Ernest Bevin, A.V. Alexander and Herbert Morrison, the next three most senior Labour Cabinet Ministers in Churchill's Coalition Government. All were agreeable to maintaining the coalition until the defeat of Japan, an event believed to be at least a year away. Attlee asked Churchill if, in his letter formally asking Labour to maintain the coalition, he could add a sentence about implementing the proposals "for social security and full employment" that had been put forward in the proposed Four-Year Plan by William Beveridge, who had been one of Churchill's main advisers on social reform legislation before the First World War. Churchill readily agreed.

Attlee then took Churchill's letter with him to Blackpool, where the Labour Party annual conference was in session. There, however, the decision to maintain an all-party Government was taken out of the Labour leaders' hands by their own rank and file, who urged a swift end to the coalition, a return to party politics, and the prospect—so long denied the Labour Party—of political power. Attlee telephoned Churchill with this news on the evening of May 21.

Just as it had been the Labour Party members' refusal to serve under Neville Chamberlain in May 1940 that propelled Churchill to the premiership, so their decision in May 1945 to insist on an immediate General Election brought his wartime coalition to an end. That demand cast a question over whether, once the votes were counted, he would remain Prime Minister.

Given the determination of the Labour Party to return to party politics, Churchill had no alternative but to dissolve the coalition, and at noon, on May 23, he went to Buckingham Palace to resign. Attlee had offered to keep the Labour Ministers in the government for another five months, but Churchill wrote to King George VI: 'It would be no service to the nation to go forward with a pretence of union which had in fact lapsed with the attainment of complete victory over Germany."

The King accepted the fact that the coalition was at an end. From that moment, Britain was plunged back into the unpredictable realm of party politics. Until a General Election could be called, Churchill remained Prime Minister at the head of an entirely Conservative administration, known as the Caretaker Government. "You know what it means to me," he wrote to Ernest Bevin, "not to have your aid in these terrible times," and, he added optimistically but in vain: "We must hope for re-union when Party passions are less strong."

The House of Commons met on May 29 with the Labour Party in opposition. With the General Election set for July 5, politicians of all colours plunged into the cut and thrust of electioneering. "Party ties have been considered honourable bonds," Churchill declared on June 4, in his first party political broadcast of the election, but a few moments later he harmed the Conservative cause when he said, with the deep foreboding that he felt: "No Socialist Government, conducting the entire life and industry of the country, could afford to allow free, sharp, or violently worded expression of public discontent. They would fall back on some form of Gestapo, no doubt very humanely directed in the first instance. And this would nip opinion in the bud; it would stop criticism as it reared its head; and it would gather all the power to the supreme Party and the Party leaders." Churchill added that "a Free Parliament is odious to the Socialist doctrinaire."

The phrase "some form of Gestapo" caused a furore. Churchill's wife had begged him not to use it.

Churchill continued campaigning. One of the disadvantages facing the Conservatives was Churchill's own long pre-war campaign against their failure to prepare Britain adequately for war. He was no longer speaking as a war leader but as head of a party he himself had spent so much time discrediting, and against a party much of whose proposed legislation drew on what he himself had supported—and brought onto the Statute Book—in his earlier years. In his second broadcast on June 13, at the suggestion of his daughter Sarah, he elaborated on Beveridge's Four-Year Plan. "I announced this to the nation two years ago," he said, "under the simple watchword of 'food, work, and homes.' Of this extensive plan as yet only education and family allowances stand on the Statute Book, and they are yet to be carried into full effect. But we have left social insurance, industrial injuries insurance, and the National Health Service to be shaped by Parliament and to be made to play a dynamic part in the life and security of every family and home."

Churchill spoke with sincerity and conviction, but the public remembered too vividly the "Gestapo speech" and looked to the Labour Party, not to the Conservatives, to move forward along the lines of social reform that Churchill so wanted. What he condemned, he said, "on the most severe terms," was the "Socialist effort to drag their long-term fads and wavy Utopias across the practical path of need and duty."

The General Election results were to be announced on July 26. Churchill flew back half way through the "Big Three" Potsdam Conference to hear them. Attlee flew back with him. The Labour Party, with 393 seats, won an absolute majority of 146 over all the other parties. The Conservative seats fell from the 585 achieved in the previous General Election in 1935 to 213. For the first time in British history, the Labour vote was higher than that of the Conservatives (11,995,152 as against

9,988,396). Clement Attlee became Prime Minister and returned to Potsdam alone to negotiate the postwar settlement with Stalin and President Harry S Truman.

The election results were an accurate reflection of party conflicts and public desires that had been in abeyance while Churchill was wartime Prime Minister. They represented a return to the free forces of public expression and the search for votes in favour of one party's program against another's. The Labour Party program of social reform—including nationalization of the railways, which Churchill had advocated twenty years earlier—helped secure a majority of the nation's votes and brought the Labour Party to power.

There was another factor that worked against a Conservative victory: the memories of its pre-war appeasement policies and neglect of Britain's defences. Lord Beaverbrook (the Canadian Max Aitken), himself a pre-war pro-appeasement Conservative, wrote to a friend when the election results were known: "The main factor in the political landslide here lies way back in the years 1938–40. It was about that time that the great mass of middle-class opinion in Britain decided to punish the Conservatives. It is unfortunate that the blows intended for the heads of Mr Chamberlain and his colleagues should fall on Mr Churchill." The unpopularity of the Conservative Party, Beaverbrook added, "proved too strong for the greatness of Churchill and the affection in which he is held by the people."

The General Election result was a clear demonstration of the procedures of parliamentary democracy at work. When Churchill's Principal Private Secretary, Leslie Rowan, spoke to him of the ingratitude of the British people, Churchill replied, "That's politics, my dear, that's politics." To his doctor, who mentioned that same word, "ingratitude" when the results were known, Churchill responded: "I wouldn't call it that. They have had a very hard time."

Defeat in no way altered Churchill's faith in democratic procedures. He neither despaired of the parliamentary process nor turned his back on it. In the words of his daughter Mary, in her biography of her mother: "Winston did not lurk long licking his wounds; when Parliament reassembled on 1st August, less than a week after the election results, he took his new place on the Opposition front bench."

On 24 August 1945, within a month of becoming Leader of the Opposition and still holding his Epping seat, later delineated as Woodford, Churchill told the House of Commons: "This House is not only a machine for legislation; perhaps it is not even mainly a machine for legislation, it is a great forum of Debate." It had to tackle the dominating issues of the day. If the House were not able "to discuss matters which the country is discussing, which fill the newspapers, which everyone is anxious and preoccupied about, it loses its contact; it is no longer marching step by step with all the thought that is in progress in the country."

Public cynicism at the parliamentary process was something Churchill always sought to combat. On 11 November 1947, nineteen days before his seventy-third birthday, he told the House of Commons: "Many forms of Government have been tried, and will be tried in this world of sin and woe . . . No one pretends that democracy is perfect or all-wise. Indeed it has been said that democracy is the worst form of government except all those other forms that have been tried from time to time." But it was democracy that was the system in which the electorate was sovereign, not the legislature. As Churchill expressed it: "It is not Parliament that should rule; it is the people who should rule through Parliament."

Churchill reiterated this theme when he spoke to the Norwegian Parliament in Oslo on 13 May 1948: "In both our lands, it is the people who control the Government, not the Government the people." As Leader of the Opposition, Churchill was then engaged, with his Conservative colleagues, in a continual struggle against the Labour Government's legislation.

One aspect of the British parliamentary system that displeased Churchill was the right of people not to vote. As he saw it, not voting was not a right but a sign of laziness or neglect, a failure to enter fully into the working of the society in which one lived. "I have a strong view," he told the House of Commons on 23 June 1948, "that voting should be compulsory, as it is in Australia and in Holland, and that there should be a small fine for people who do not choose to exercise their civic duty."

Another strong view Churchill held concerned the actual structure of the House of Commons. In maintaining the parliamentary system, Churchill saw particular merit in the physical nature of the debating Chamber of the House of Commons. It had been built in such a way that, by 1900, there was not enough room on the benches for more than two-thirds of the Members to find a place to sit. As a result, during important debates, many Members had to stand, emphasizing the sense of urgency and attentiveness. The Chamber, having been destroyed during a German air raid in 1941, was restored in 1950. Many people thought that the new Chamber should have room on the benches for every Member.

In this debate, Churchill supported the return to the pre-war arrangement. As he told the House of Commons on 24 October 1950:

It excites world wonder in the Parliamentary countries that we should build a Chamber, starting afresh, which can only seat two-thirds of its Members. It is difficult to explain this to those who do not know our ways. They cannot easily be made to understand why we consider that the intensity, passion, intimacy, informality and spontaneity of our Debates constitute the personality of the House of Commons and endow it at once with its focus and its strength . . . it is the champion of the people against executive oppression . . . the House of Commons has ever been the controller, and if need be, the changer of the rulers of the day and of the Ministers appointed by the Crown. It stands for every man against the oligarchy and one-man power . . . The House of Commons stands for freedom and law, and this is the message which the Mother of Parliaments has proved herself capable of proclaiming to the world at large.

Churchill was convinced that the pre-war structure should be retained—that in times of crisis or emergency, an overpacked Chamber gave credence to the urgency of the moment. In all other parliamentary assemblies in the world, where every Member has a seat, it is much harder to gain a sense of crisis from the actual disposition of Members around the Chamber. Churchill's view prevailed. The rebuilt Chamber, like the old, has insufficient seats for all its Members, thereby enhancing, as Churchill saw it, the democratic nature of the parliamentary scene.

Twelve years earlier, on 18 December 1938, in an article in the *News of the World,* Churchill had written of how he had been in many legislatures of the world, "but I have never seen one in which I should care to make a speech." He had seen so many foreign assemblies "where they all sit in a semi-circle, and everyone has a place, or even a desk, which he can bang when he is displeased, and where each speaker goes up to a pulpit to harangue an audience scattered through a large area." Churchill's experience and perspective was clear: "The essential of keen debate is the sense of a crowd, clustering together craning forward, gathering round the speaker, with the cheers and counter-cheers flung back from side to side." It was this quality that was preserved in the rebuilding of the Chamber in 1950.

———

For almost six years, Churchill was Leader of the Opposition. He insisted throughout in maintaining a balance of criticism. He saw no virtue in criticism for its own sake, believing that parliamentary democracy should allow for a sense of common purpose whenever that was offered. Thus he would not allow his party to oppose the India Independence Bill—feeling that independence should be the gift of the whole House, not of one Party—and he supported Clement Attlee's introduction of National Military Service to meet the demands of the Korean War, a United Nations' enterprise.

Such cooperation did not mean that Churchill did not also see the House of Commons as the essential forum for the sharpest of criticisms. On 12 September 1950 he told the House, in defence of the strong Conservative criticisms of government policy: "Both Governments and Oppositions have responsibilities to discharge, but they are a different order. The Government, with their whole control over our executive power, have the burden and the duty . . . to make sure that the safety of the country is provided for; the shape, formation, and the direction of policy is in their hands alone. The responsibilities of the Opposition are limited to aiding the Government in the measures which we agree are for national safety and also to criticizing and correcting . . . any errors and shortcomings which may be apparent, but the Opposition are not responsible for proposing integrated and complicated measures of policy."

One change that had begun in the 1930s was not to Churchill's taste but, by 1950, had become too integral a part of parliamentary procedure to change. This was the Committee system, whereby much legislation was discussed in various committees before it came to the floor of the House. On 1 January 1939 he had written, in the *News of the World:* "Sometimes, when the Chamber itself is almost empty, as many as two hundred members are gathered in a big Committee room upstairs, debating with earnestness and vivacity the very topics that ought to be discussed upon the Floor." This system "was upon the whole unhealthy." It is still in place today, however, half a century after Churchill's active life in the House of Commons ended.

As the Labour Government struggled to maintain its majority, the political battle intensified. At the General Election on 23 February 1950, Labour was returned to power with a greatly decreased majority—its seats falling from 393 to 315 and the Conservative seats rising from 213 to 298—an overall Labour majority, discounting the Speaker, of only six. Churchill, who earlier had recommended a five-year gap between General Elections, pressed for another election as soon as possible. As he told the House of Commons on 6 November 1950: "We must not forget what votes are. Votes are the means by which the poorest people in the country and all the people in the country can make sure that they get their vital needs attended to."

The second General Election within two years was held on 25 October 1951. Although the actual number of votes cast for Labour (13,948,605) were slightly higher than those cast for the Conservatives (13,717,538), the constituency system of "first past the post" ensured 321 Conservative seats against 295 for Labour. Churchill became Prime Minister for a second time.

The election result led to an upsurge in calls for proportional representation, on the assumption that Labour would have won the election if such a system had been in place. Churchill commented in the House of Commons on 17 February 1953: "It is quite true that I expressed a view many years ago, which I have not seen any reason to dismiss from the region of theoretical principle, in favour of proportional representation in great cities. I have not expressed any views in favour of proportional representation as a whole, on account of the proved ill-effect it has on so many Parliaments." Speaking in general about opinions he had once held, but held no longer, he told the House of Commons on 5 May 1952: "My views are a harmonious process, which keeps them in relation to the current movement of events."

———

One aspect of parliamentary democracy that Churchill held as central to the working of the whole system was the Monarchy as compared to a Presidency. "There is no doubt," he said on 7 February 1952, in his broadcast tribute after the death of King George VI, "that of all the institutions which have grown up among us over the centuries, or sprung into being in our lifetime, the constitutional monarchy is the most deeply founded and dearly cherished by the whole association of our peoples. In the present generation it has acquired a meaning incomparably more powerful than anyone had dreamed possible in former times. The Crown has become the mysterious link—indeed, I may say, the magic link—which unites our loosely bound but strongly interwoven Commonwealth of Nations, States and races. Peoples who would never tolerate the assertions of a written constitution, which implied any diminution of their independence, are the foremost to be proud of their loyalty to the Crown."

From his first visit to the United States in 1895, Churchill had made fourteen visits across the Atlantic before the end of his second premiership in 1955. He had met several American Presidents, starting with William McKinley in 1900, and he often reflected on the contrast between the parliamentary and the presidential systems. Jock Colville, his Joint Principal Private Secretary in his second premiership, later commented on Churchill's attitude to the American presidential system: "He was firmly opposed both to a presidential system and to the separation of powers." Colville went on to quote Churchill's warning: "The union of the pomp and the power of the State in a single office exposes a mortal to strains beyond the nature, and to tasks beyond the strength, even of the best and greatest of men."

There was another outside factor that Churchill believed was important in the maintenance of parliamentary democracy—the Parliamentary Press, the journalists with their special place in the Chamber overlooking the debates from the gallery and reporting on them. On 28 October 1952, a year after returning to power,

Churchill told the House of Commons that the Parliamentary Press "has a most important function to discharge, which is to give a fair and truthful report of what passes in the House of Commons." And, he added, with his familiar verbal twinkle: "That does not mean that everyone has to write the same truth; as Mr. Baldwin said, it may be approached from so many angles." He was, however, concerned, telling the House: "In my lifetime I have seen the reporting of the debates in Parliament shrink a great deal as a factor in our public life. Far less space is now given in the newspaper. I know there is a shortage of newsprint, but apart from that, I do not think people give to Parliament the same attention as they used to do."

It was the parliamentary system of elections that Churchill prized. As he told Members of Parliament on 3 November 1953: "Elections exist for the sake of the House of Commons, and not the House of Commons for the sake of elections."

On his eightieth birthday—30 November 1954—while still Prime Minister, Churchill was honoured by both Houses of Parliament. In his speech accepting their congratulations, he declared: "I have lived in the House of Commons, having service there for fifty-two of the fifty-four years of this tumultuous and convulsive century. . . .

I have never ceased to love the Mother of Parliaments, the model to the legislative assemblies of so many lands." Churchill spoke these words during what his daughter Mary, in her biography of her mother, called "the moving, and in parliamentary history unique, ceremony" when both Houses of Parliament assembled in Westminster Hall to pay their tribute to him.

There was to be one more example of Churchill's parliamentary skills and his recourse to Parliament for matters that were urgent. On 1 March 1955 he impressed the House of Commons by the vigour of his words and thoughts on the hydrogen bomb, in what his daughter Mary has called a "momentous and magisterial" speech. Churchill's proposal in that speech was to use the existence of the hydrogen bomb, and its deterrent power, as the basis for world disarmament.

Churchill resigned as Prime Minister in April 1955. He remained a Member of Parliament for another nine years, unable, with increasing age and infirmity, to take part in the debates but attending as much as possible. His last appearance, when he was eighty-nine years old, was on 27 July 1964, sixty-three years after he had first taken his seat. The General Election of October 1964 was the first he had not contested since 1900.

Parliament had been Churchill's active platform and base for more than half a century. With pride he had called himself "a child of the House of Commons." Even as a schoolboy, the conflicts and struggles of parliamentary democracy had impinged on his home life. His biography of his father, published after Churchill had been in the House of Commons for only six years, reflected his understanding of the parliamentary battles of the nineteenth century. From the start of the twentieth century, he had made his own strongly individual contribution to the working of Parliament and to its legislation.

Churchill was a great respecter of the rules and conventions of political life. He even observed the formality—twice in his career, in 1904 and 1925—of crossing the floor of the House from one set of party benches to another: "Anyone can rat," he once said, "but it takes courage to re-rat." He had a clear conviction that the conflict of party philosophies and actions should be encouraged as an integral part of parliamentary democracy. "Party conflict and Party government should not be disparaged," he wrote in his war memoirs. "It is in time of peace, and when national safety is not threatened, one of those conditions of a free Parliamentary democracy for which no permanent substitute is known."

Even in wartime Churchill held this view, telling the House of Commons on 13 September 1943: "Party government is not obnoxious to democracy. Indeed Parliamentary democracy has flourished under Party government." There were, of course, limits to the vigour of parliamentary debate. As he told his fellow parliamentarians on 6 June 1951: "The object of Parliament is to substitute for fisticuffs." This was a simple but true description of what differentiated parliamentary democracy from tyranny and dictatorship. Eight months earlier, on 24 October 1950, during the debate on the rebuilding of the Chamber in its pre-war form, Churchill said of the House of Commons: "It is the champion of the people against executive oppression," and he went on to explain what he meant. The House of Commons "has ever been the controller and, if need be, the changer of the rulers of the day and of Ministers appointed by the Crown. It stands forever against oligarchy and one-man power."

As peacetime Prime Minister, Churchill remained concerned with every aspect of the complex fabric of the methods and traditions of the House of Commons. On 15 November 1951, in defending the Speaker of the House for his interventions at times of unruly debates and interruptions, he declared: "In these hard Party fights under democratic conditions, as in football matches and the like, there are moments when the umpire gets a very rough time." The Speaker, he explained, "represents and embodies the spirit of the House of Commons and that spirit, which has transported itself to so many lands and climates and to countries far outside our sphere, is one of the gleaming and enduring glories of the British and in a special way . . . of the English message to the world."

It was not only in Britain that Churchill saw and admired the working of parliamentary democracy. It flourished in the former Dominions, most notably in

Canada, Australia and New Zealand. It prevailed in India, which, with its population of more than a billion in the opening years of the twenty-first century, can boast that it is the world's largest democracy. "All these traditions," Churchill said in his speech of 24 October 1950, ". . . have brought us into being over hundreds of years, carrying a large proportion of the thought of the human race with us, as these traditions received new draughts of life as the franchise was extended until it became universal. The House of Commons stands for freedom and law, and this is the message which the Mother of Parliaments has proved itself capable of proclaiming to the world at large."

The place that parliamentary democracy had, and still has, in maintaining the rights of man in civic society in many nations cannot be sustained and preserved by lip service alone. As Churchill's lifelong association and involvement in the parliamentary process shows, it has to be believed in, nourished and fought for—sometimes literally fought for on the battlefield—against those who wish to destroy it. It requires permanent, active, positive support—on the floor of the Parliament, on public platforms, and in the hearts and minds of those whose lives and way of life it protects and enhances.

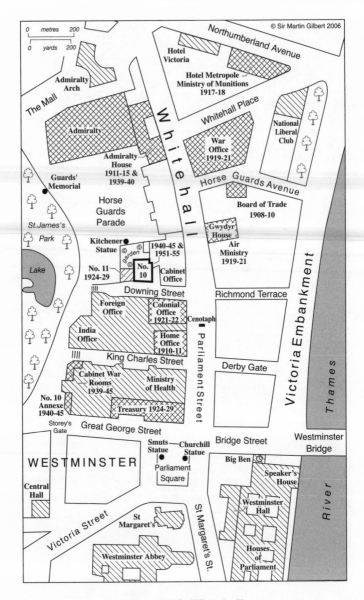

0 metres 200

0 yards 200

Northumberland Avenue

The Mall

Admiralty Arch

Hotel Victoria

Hotel Metropole
Ministry of Munitions
1917-18

Whitehall Place

Admiralty

Admiralty
House
1911-15 &
1939-40

War
Office
1919-21

National
Liberal
Club

W h i t e h a l l

Horse Guards Avenue

Guards'
Memorial

Horse
Guards
Parade

Board of Trade
1908-10

St.James's
Park

Gwydyr
House

Lake

Kitchener
Statue

1940-45 &
1951-55

garden

No.
10

Cabinet
Office

Air
Ministry
1919-21

No. 11
1924-29

Downing Street

Richmond Terrace

Foreign
Office

Colonial
Office
1921-22

Cenotaph

India
Office

Home
Office
1910-11

Parliament Street

King Charles Street

Derby Gate

Cabinet War
Rooms
1939-45

Ministry
of Health

Victoria Embankment

No. 10
Annexe
1940-45

Treasury 1924-29

T h a m e s

Storey's
Gate

Great George Street

Bridge Street

Westminster
Bridge

Smuts
Statue

Churchill
Statue

WESTMINSTER

Parliament
Square

Big Ben

Speaker's
House

Central
Hall

R i v e r

Victoria Street

St
Margaret's

St Margaret's St.

Westminster
Hall

Westminster Abbey

Houses
of
Parliament

Churchill's Whitehall

Places in Great Britain mentioned in this book

Acknowledgements

The origin of this book was a lecture I gave in Toronto in 2003 to the Churchill Society for the Advancement of Parliamentary Democracy. A previous lecture to the society had been given by Sir John Colville, Winston Churchill's former Joint Principal Private Secretary and friend. It was Colville who helped me over many years to understand Churchill's work and ideas—and his ideals.

I am grateful to Anne Collins, Esther Goldberg, Michael Levine, Andrew McMurtry and Kay Thomson, who have encouraged me to examine Churchill's view and practice of parliamentary democracy and whose collective enthusiasm has enabled this book to take shape.

November 16, 2005

Note on Sources

Churchill's speeches and statements in the House of Commons cited here are taken from *Hansard,* the official parliamentary record. Sir John Colville's reflections are taken from the speech he gave in Toronto on

26 November 1986 to a joint meeting of the Empire Club of Canada and the Churchill Society for the Advancement of Parliamentary Democracy. All other quotations, unless otherwise indicated in the text, are from the eight main and sixteen document volumes of *Winston S. Churchill* by Randolph Churchill (1874–1914) and Martin Gilbert (1914–65), and from Martin Gilbert's single-volume *Churchill, A Life*.

Index

MARTIN GILBERT

Sir Martin Gilbert is Winston Churchill's official biographer, and a leading historian of the modern world. He is the author of seventy-six books, among them the single-volume *Churchill: A Life*, his much-acclaimed twin histories, *First World War* and *Second World War*, a comprehensive *History of Israel*, and his three-volume *History of the Twentieth Century*. He is an Honorary Fellow of Merton College, Oxford, and a Distinguished Fellow of Hillsdale College, Michigan. His website is www.martingilbert.com